REAL
PROCUREMENT
TRANSFORMATION

POWERFUL, SUSTAINING

ALAN HUSTWICK

Tellwell Talent
www.tellwell.ca

ISBN
978-0-2288-6270-3 (Paperback)
978-0-2288-7700-4 (eBook)

TABLE OF CONTENTS

PREFACE

I enjoy teaching, coaching, knowledge sharing, and watching people grow in their roles and progress in their careers. In the last half of my business career, I specialised in procurement, and I discovered that I became passionate about the subject, its impact on business performance, its wider strategic potential as well as the intellectual challenges presented. I now want to share my experience with the broader global procurement community to revolutionise the profession to a standard of uniform excellence. That is what this book is all about.

For this reason, I have decided to expand on my earlier published book, *Procurement — Redefined, Impactful, Compelling,* and provide the reader with hands-on tools, supported by illustrations, commentary and practical advice to achieve successful procurement transformation and deliver sustained, superior value as a top-performing team. This book complements the first and goes deeper. It will provide the reader with an expanded suite of protocols to support the change agenda, drive simplification and deliver superior value. It is more specialised in its content, namely *transformation,* to lift procurement's performance. As a former colleague of mine described it, my first book is about the architecture— the design of procurement excellence — while this book is more about the engineering drawings, the *how-to* that can be used to implement and embed change.

Procurement professionals will be well aware much has been written on the subject of transformation. In fact, *transformation* has become an overused expression and means different things to different people. I use the word *transformation* to indicate a changed procurement approach that generates three important and visible outcomes. These are:

- simplified processes including organisational structure, protocols and governance that collectively define and are the foundations for excellence in procurement

- raising the profile of procurement within the business to an elevated status and one respected as the leading commercial team in the organisation

- to drive rapid and sustained cost reduction and other metrics sharply aligned with organisational financial and strategic performance.

It may take just one of these drivers to achieve all three. For example, if procurement leads cost reduction activity in an organisation driven by an urgency to turn around its financial performance, then simplification in documentation and process will be a prerequisite. Further, if procurement is successful in meeting the turnaround challenge presented, its higher status is guaranteed.

Excellence in procurement is the outcome that transformation brings. In the following chapters, I describe what excellence looks like — the outcome of a challenging and rewarding journey. Rather than starting with a definition of excellence through metrics and other indicators, it is the *journey to get there* that is the critical part of the process to ensure all benefits are sustained. It is important to get the necessary fundamentals in place and know what is involved in the journey so that required planning can be done and executed.

To aid this change journey and understanding of key concepts, I use graphical presentations that are easy to absorb. They are supported by a narrative based on practical experience that explains the intent and purpose of each, which cumulatively leads to and supports outcomes intended by transformation objectives.

The primary aim of the book, therefore, is to describe **how** a procurement team can progress or transform from their current status to a leadership position and one respected by their organisation, their peer group, and also be a team measured by improvement to key business metrics. It outlines the necessary prerequisites that are required to be in place before embarking on major change. It also provides the **what** so that readers can immediately adopt protocols for use in practice as well as necessary communication that describes to users and business leaders the details and rationale for change.

My intended audience is broad. It includes senior leadership who are authorised to set the organisational context, to drive and support change, as well as procurement leadership and professionals charged with implementation of practice and adoption into the workplace. Additionally, the book can be used as a learning and development resource by anyone in procurement teams, regardless of level, who desires to learn, grow, challenge the status quo, and influence outcomes that lead to a better business.

Readers may be familiar with the business jargon, *definition of insanity*. Simply put, it refers to doing the same thing over and over again and expecting different results. With specific reference to procurement, retaining the same processes, procedures and systems cannot result in any step-change in improvement unless these are changed. This book helps procurement teams in that journey.

A fair question that needs to be asked is, *"Why* am I so passionate to write this book and promote transformational change in procurement practice?" The answer is simple. The leverage and impact a high-performing procurement team can have on an organisation are huge if the team has the right processes, technology and custody of its external spend. This is in comparison to a typical team heavily focused on process, providing a service to the business, and measured on a primary metric of price that has no direct visibility with business performance.

I worked in a major global corporation for twenty-five years in a number of finance, commercial and procurement roles. The work was always challenging, rewarding and fulfilling. Interestingly, my time in procurement roles had two very different experiences. Both were rigorous in their approach, had structure, used defined processes, respected key governance principles, and delivered commercial outcomes. Both added value in the eyes of stakeholders.

On reflection, I would describe my first experience as consistent with a Tier 1 approach to procurement typically adopted by large organisations, a service level organisation, rigorous in process compliance, governance and adherence to protocols. There was heavy reliance on Request for Proposal (RFP) and Tender documentation. The primary metric was on price, usually determined by ensuring a minimum of three competitive responses for every source program. In other words, what I would describe as traditional procurement, typically adopted by most businesses and organisations. The second experience was provided through a rare opportunity to be a leader in a business turnaround scenario, where typical procurement methodologies deployed and described above would take too long to deliver the rapid cost reduction required in the timeframe allowed to achieve business survival. That naturally necessitated change in process, given the speed to deliver required outcomes. In practice, it is substantially no different from what a Tier 2 business would adopt, namely, smaller organisations that cannot afford nor desire heavy corporate structures. Lean, mean and outcome-focused.

As a footnote, the turnaround objectives were achieved and did use much-simplified procurement processes.

The experience was not only a beneficial one but having gone through it made me realise these practices not only deliver better commercial outcomes they also represent good business. It is that experience I share in this book. It is practical in focus and provides a differentiated approach and thinking. My style is an engaging one so it is written in language for readers to understand.

Readers who have read my first book would know I challenge the status quo, conventional wisdom and traditional processes typically adopted by procurement organisations. I continue with this approach for the reasons noted above and advise on practices that drive outcomes sharply aligned with business strategy. I also promote a fresh and different perspective that raises procurement to a top-line and high visibility team in the business.

As further context to this book, which I discuss more deeply in the next and following chapters, is a challenge I want to put to the procurement community: "Do you know what you don't know?" Or, to put it another way, "Do you know what procurement excellence looks like, its definition, the full scale of benefits it can bring to a business and where you stand in relation to it?" The point of raising this is to say that real improvement can only come from understanding there is a gap, acknowledging it, and having a strong commitment to achieving the desired outcome. Procurement is a fast-moving profession, and what was good twenty years ago has changed substantially, albeit some elements remain. Even if you cannot answer the question, an independent gap assessment may open up the true potential a high-performing procurement team can deliver to the business. Adopting a transformation agenda provides that opportunity.

This book should be read by all procurement professionals and business leaders as it provides the keys to support significant organisational improvement in financial and commercial performance.

CHAPTER 1

Setting the Context

This book is about *change*. Specifically, how to change from a low visibility/customer service orientated and price-focused procurement team to a high achieving one, whose value is measured by metrics consistent with key business performance and strategic direction. It will be respected as the *key* resource to drive commercial value and be held in high regard by all levels of the organisation.

Let me start by asking a question. I will assume you are either in a procurement role or interface with procurement as a customer or leader of the function. In other words, you know what a procurement team does. The question is, "What is your procurement team's value proposition?" Or, to put it another way, "How does your procurement team add value to the organisation?"

Answers will vary, but I would suggest they will be "we buy goods and services for the business," or adding the words, "for the best value the market provides and in accordance with customer requirements." Some answers may include these words and add an extra dimension, "we further assure a supply chain service to ensure all goods and materials are available to meet business needs."

The challenge I pose to these responses is that if procurement is charged with sourcing, negotiating and contractually agreeing to an organisation's external spend base, none of these answers align with strategic business direction or contribute to growth in shareholder value. No other team in the business has the capability to underpin or drive this objective. Therefore, if that is to become procurement's new mandate, its status will need to rise and operate in a peer capacity with finance, production and marketing to influence, drive and embed short and long-term business goals.

Procurement, though, cannot move to a high achieving team acting alone, but if the will, desire, drive and commitment are there, it will succeed. It will require passionate and committed leadership. What this book describes and provides readers is how to progress to this aspiration and subscribe to the following value proposition, "Procurement is the key and respected organisation resource that secures goods, services and materials to the organisation aligned with key business performance metrics, strategic objectives, priorities and values. It is the primary commercial team in the business."

The assumption I am making is that you want to operate at this level. I am assuming you have the motivation but are not sure how to get there or have tried to do so before and failed. Alternatively, you are in a business that does not value procurement and seek directional breakthrough guidance to take you there. Then, I offer a pathway to take you there.

The key resource to aid this transformation, as it is for any major organisational change, is the company's Chief Executive Officer (CEO). With their support and endorsement, the requisite authority exists as the CEO is accountable for strategic direction, company-wide cost reduction programs, and change in organisational structures and mandates. Above all, the CEO will want to ensure the outcome is successful, particularly if the proposed strategic outcome leads to a significant increase in shareholder value, as procurement transformation would. You can be assured such a proposition will resonate with them and command their attention.

It is at this juncture, though, that we should press the 'pause' button. We should consider *why* this support is essential, whether the necessary preparation required is ready for this high-level engagement, and whether the requisite sponsorship is there to proceed.

You need to be ready for the CEO discussion and with *transformation* in mind. A clear strategy should be developed focusing on where you want to take the business, constraints to the current practices identified, and key changes required to the procurement operating model and processes. This needs to be supported by an implementation plan, including how it will be resourced, the strategic business benefits and when these benefits will accrue to the organisation. The presentation should be short, to the point and capable of delivery in thirty minutes, plus an allowance for questions. Of particular importance is the Implementation Plan to achieve the desired outcome as if it is short in substance, this will be quickly identified and delay the start of the initiative.

I noted in the preceding paragraph the phrase, *operating model*. Simply put, an operating model is the bridge between strategy and day-to-day operations that guides the procurement team, provides the context, and enables the team to deliver on the strategy and vision. It is *how* a business using people, process and technology deliver value articulated in the strategy. It would typically cover what work is done and how, the service provided, by whom, control points and key governance requirements, as well as how decisions are made and authority levels of key stakeholders. It would also include a scorecard for assessing performance. What I describe is only a light touch on the subject, and a quick internet search will show all Tier 1 consulting firms offering much more detail on the subject, and for that reason, I have kept the definition short.

Resources applied to transformation should have the required capability to execute the work. Protocols will require development, or as a minimum, changed to align with procurement's new strategic direction, as existing protocols may only be relevant to 'old' ways of doing business. There needs to be a level of investment in technology. Moreover, the strategy requires four further essential requirements to be in place. These are listed below and explain why the CEO endorsement is essential.

The first is the organisational *culture* must be aligned with procurement's strategic aims, which in turn should be consistent with business strategy. This is particularly important as one key outcome of transformation is to enable substantial cost reduction to place the business in a sound, competitive position. Operations will need to be aware of key changes to procurement's operating model and cost reduction targets. Otherwise, they will have no incentive or appetite to accept commercial options presented for review and acceptance. For example, there may be a level of risk required (new supplier, new product) to achieve a lower cost outcome, and without context, rejection is likely. In other words, if cost reduction is the priority, everyone in the business should feel the hunger and necessity to achieve lower costs, incentivised to do so and agnostic of supplier selection. Only the CEO has the authority to set this context. Even if cost reduction is not the primary driver, changes to the operating model will require education, training and support to ensure successful implementation.

The second requirement is adoption of equal *measures* applied to each business team. Procurement should adopt measures aligned with key business metrics, equal to Operations and other teams. No one group should have authority over the other, and all teams are unified to achieve one outcome, namely, improved business performance through all sources, including procurement's leverage. By necessity, therefore, procurement now focuses on measurable business outcomes as the primary driver of value and not exclusively on price and process compliance. Adopting these measures of performance will have a further major benefit in that procurement shifts from being a service provider to one fully integrated into the business. The third requirement is to ensure progress towards achieving strategic outcomes are *measured and reported* to an oversight body chaired by the CEO or direct reports, showing actual performance as well as forecast for the remainder of the financial period. Strict project management discipline should be applied, holding resources to account in both value and timing.

Lastly, only the CEO has the vested authority to set priorities for the business. If procurement transformation and cost reduction are a priority, then the organisation needs to be informed by senior leadership. In that way, the business exercises *demand pull* behaviours, engaging procurement to support them in achievement of cost reduction. This is instead of *procurement push,* convincing the business to adopt new commercial outcomes or new suppliers, which in my experience rarely works because the business has no incentive to absorb lower costs and potentially higher risk as production will always be paramount to Operations.

Not all elements in a procurement strategy that takes the business to a new higher level of operating require CEO input and endorsement. It would be necessary for the Chief Procurement Officer (CPO) to design and implement key process changes and supporting protocols to achieve simplification and alignment with strategic business direction. For example, if a key aspect of business strategy is to achieve a major cost reduction target within a defined timeframe, relying on long, complex Tender and Request for Proposal (RFP) documentation will not serve the purpose. RFPs need to be shortened, with governance and contractual matters separated out from commercial requirements to enable tight timeframes to be met. Similarly, other documentation such as Request for Information (RFI) and Recommendation to Award (RTA) will require simplification. Once done, it will be very hard to revert to old ways of working, as removing time-consuming bureaucratic and expensive processes have no place in a modern business environment. Key governance aspects are still necessary, but by enhancing a company's website and providing a Procurement tab listing supplier qualification requirements, suppliers can self-qualify on key assurance aspects. Having this in place will greatly simplify execution of sourcing programs and allow procurement's primary focus to be on pure commercial aspects.

Additionally, new measures of performance require definition and alignment with business outcomes, not on process compliance. For example, measures such as "# of sourcing programs executed" or "% of goods under contract" have no relevance to the hard metrics of business performance, albeit they may still have a place on a procurement team board. In the following chapter, I encourage the adoption of the Total Cost Impact (TCI) measure so that commercial outcomes can be easily traced to the company's financial statements. That will place procurement equal with other C-suite executives who are incentivised to achieve core financial business metrics, and as noted, places procurement as a team integrated with the business and not as a service provider subservient to Operations.

Consideration also needs to be given to ensuring the CPO's team is resourced with people capable of executing the strategy, having the right skill set to communicate with and influence all levels in the business. These are new requirements and are not typically found in many procurement teams. An injection of new talent may be required.

In the Preface, I related my experience working for a business turnaround project which inspired this book. As noted, I gained a lot from that time. There were many positive personal benefits, but two, in particular, I want to share because they explain why transformation can change and enhance the role of a procurement professional. These are, firstly, the adoption of TCI as the primary metric of value and incentive programs, which in turn, requires a deep business understanding and personal incentive to improve bottom-line organisational performance. The pursuit of best commercial outcomes becomes relentless. It is as though you become a major shareholder or owner of the business.

Many procurement professionals will be familiar with the acronym TCO (Total Cost of Ownership), a different concept from TCI. TCO is a relevant measure and is useful when comparing two similar products, each with a different price. One may be more expensive but may provide extended product life and be better for the intended application than the cheaper alternative. The second benefit is questioning why and how adoption of a Tier 1 procurement approach is better than one focused on simplicity, speed and delivering superior commercial outcomes to all internal stakeholders as well as suppliers who value quick turnaround in decision making. I could never revert to a process-heavy Tier 1 approach as I struggle to articulate the benefits. Strategic Sourcing, once considered leading practice, is an outdated process. It is not only predictable within the supply community with documentation usually long and complex, but it is also expensive and time-consuming to run. It is a blunt instrument with limited value. However, there are simplified ways to engage the supply base to generate a market competitive outcome as explained in Chapter 5.

Finally, and along with redesign of protocols, communication requires to be taken to a new level. Once the CEO has endorsed strategy and authorised a change in procurement focus, communication needs to be aligned with a CEO's level of work, business priorities and focus. It needs to be short and impactful.

It will become evident at this stage that a substantial level of change is required to achieve and succeed in transformation. New processes, different standards of reporting and changed protocols are only a part of the change. These and more are all explained in the following chapters.

To guide you through the book, a diagram of the Transformation Wheel is below, which elaborates on what I have written above and shows six essential elements that form the glue to make transformation successful. A separate chapter is devoted to each of the six elements and follows the wheel in a clockwise direction. It is worth noting that each of the six elements is essential to ensure successful transformation, and it is not possible to cherry-pick and assume that some are discretionary; *all* require to be in place. I have covered the example above with the CEO engagement. I wrote earlier of the need to redefine processes to meet business transformation needs and rapid cost reduction. A further example I have witnessed is that if resources assigned are not up to the task of transformation, but this remains an organisational goal, there may be continued reliance on consulting firms to fill the gap, which through experience, does not lead to sustainability of outcome.

PROCUREMENT TRANSFORMATION
A MODEL

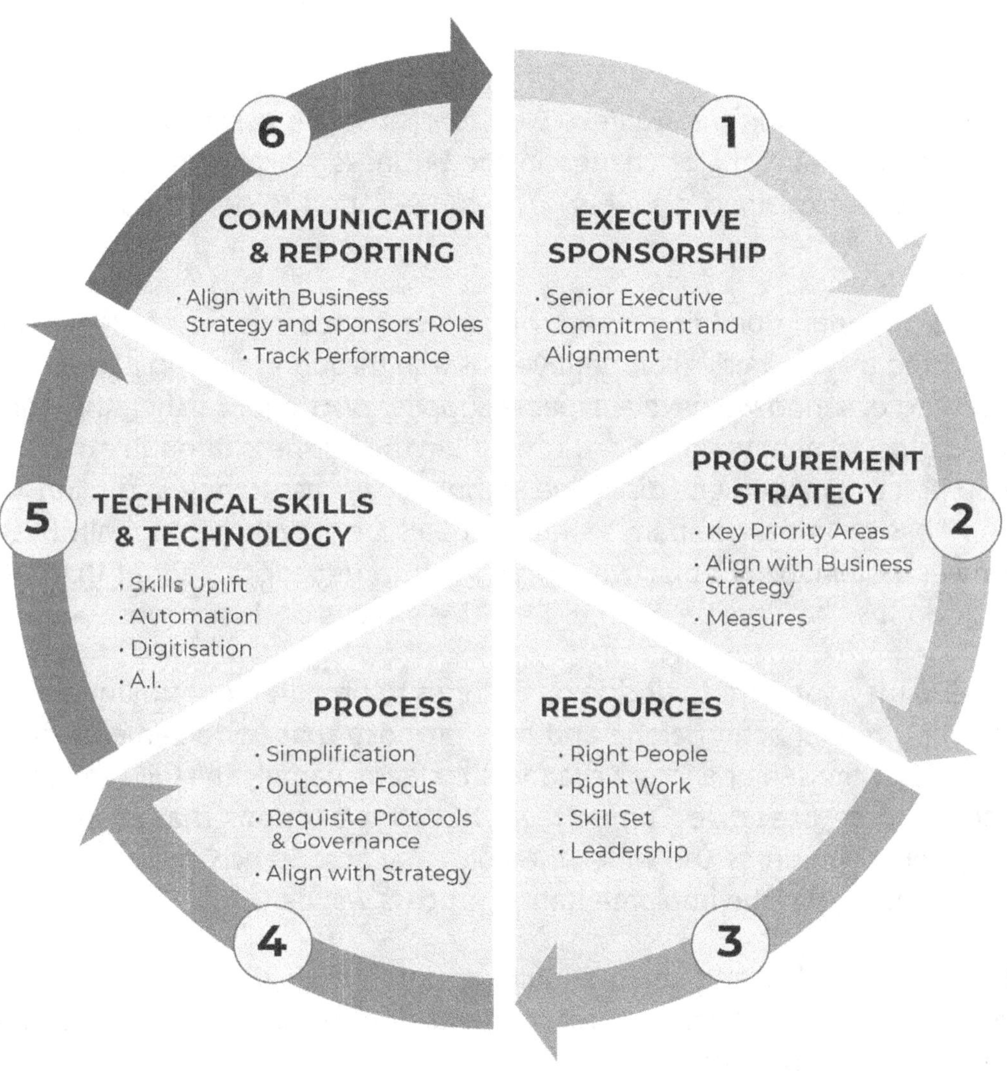

CHAPTER 2

Executive Sponsorship

In Chapter 1, *Setting the Context,* we found that the essential prerequisite for introducing any major change in the business starts with the CEO. The reasons were explained, and it is not a conversation to be feared, quite the contrary.

We are promoting building a better business, increasing shareholder value, enhancing the business's competitive position through securing a lower cost base, and ensuring we have a capable supplier portfolio. Further, through a skilled procurement team, we can strengthen the business through excellence in contract management discipline, supply chain assurance and align our supply base with the company's strategic goals, be they technologically based or meet sustainability objectives. What's not to get excited about that? The CEO's door will always be open to hear these types of discussions.

The CEO may not want to decide on changes to procurement's mandate and operating model acting alone and may propose that endorsement should be made by the senior executive leadership team, namely the CEO and direct reports, so an Executive Committee (EXCO) type forum. That is, in fact, a preferable solution as the wider the company acceptance and support for change, the easier the implementation process will be.

Naturally, the CPO and team should go into these discussions not only prepared with content and clear recommendations but also with consideration to the following two aspects:

- careful thought and practice to the opening statement, ensuring it grabs the attention of the audience, is compelling and interesting, and resonates with the work of their roles.

- knowing the audience and identifying the three most difficult questions that are likely to be asked, and answering them with confidence and fluently.

Material that should be developed for this discussion includes:

- summary and relevant extracts from the (re)developed procurement strategy (refer to Chapter 3)

- a burning platform statement — the *why*. As noted above, this should excite the audience, articulate the positive business impact, and be delivered with confidence to show you are the right team to manage and deliver the outcomes

- summary of key changes to the operating model. It would be important to show key improvements, simplification measures and other key business benefits

- project plan and timeframe to deliver

- identified risks and challenges. These should be noted as they will highlight areas where EXCO support can be provided

- conclusion and next steps

The key is to gain their endorsement. In my experience, if this comes too easily, then perhaps EXCO may have not fully grasped what is required, or maybe you have not explained fully what is expected of them. It is too easy for procurement to be told, "Of course, we support you. Just carry on and let us know if you need any help." By default, what will transpire is a *procurement push* exercise where procurement does all the work, and the business continues to believe procurement is a service provider and Operations has the right of veto over commercial recommendations. It is critical that executive leadership understand what role they have to play in procurement transformation (as explained in the previous chapter), the new authorities procurement has, the implications of the new operating model, and why the executive team must be fully engaged and provide the groundwork in the business to support and drive this change.

On the positive side, with this step on the journey complete, the real journey can begin. This is the fun part because value opportunities will be open to procurement that were not there before.

To emphasise this point further, a publication by Bain and Company, *Building a World-Class Procurement Organization* (October 2014, p.2), quoted a client reference embarking on overhauling its global procurement organisation. Their presentation began with a slide bearing three simple words to manage expectations, "Bumpy Road Ahead." Not knowing what roadblocks to expect, the team knew they would not succeed without preparing all stakeholders for the rugged journey ahead since success required unwavering commitment and support from a few leaders. They went on to say that without the necessary top-level support, it may not be worth starting the journey. Having top-level sponsorship is therefore critical.

Two useful illustrations to help deliver the message and explain to senior leadership key aspects are presented in the next pages:

PROCUREMENT PUSH V PULL

 PUSH	 PULL
· Procurement Lead	· Business Lead
· As a service provider, procurement presents commercial options to the business for acceptance / rejection	· Driven by achieving business metrics

· Option rejection driven by:
 	
  – Incompatibility of performance measures
 	
  – Procurement's subservient status to Operations
 	
  – No incentive to accept risk – change in supplier or specification
 	
  – Lack of deep engagement (Procurement / Operations) prior to sourcing (e.g., aligning strategy, BATNAs, Award Criteria)
 	
  – Operations having preferred suppliers
	· Uses procurement as a key resource to meet outcomes and targets:
	
	  – Financial
	
	  – Operational
	
	  – Supplier alignment
	
	· Treats procurement as an equal partner / resource in the business
	
	· Seeks procurement help to identify value opportunities to meet changes in specifications, service levels and other value metrics
	
	· Uses procurement as the primary commercial team to develop strategy and support implementation

SUMMARY OF KEY CHANGES

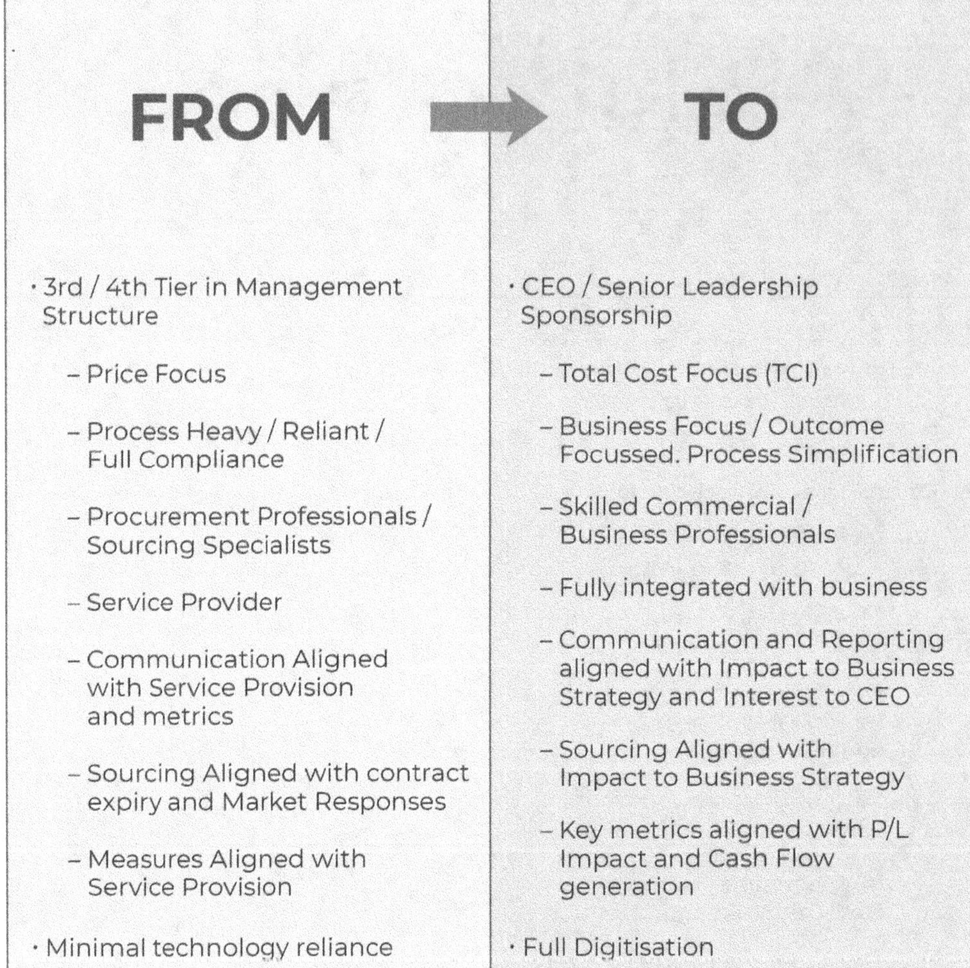

The right-hand side of both these images explains the environment that procurement is seeking to create in the business. Leadership will resonate with the left-hand side, as that will be typical of what is found in most organisations today. The task is to explain (as described above) the environment required for successful transformation and the role that leadership has to play. Their support is essential, so preparation for the discussion will be vital.

Before I leave this chapter, there is one point I wish to emphasise to round this discussion off and is of significance to the CPO in their task of Transformation.

With the accountability of the successful delivery of procurement transformation and all the many business benefits that flow from it, the CPO requires the necessary role vested authorities to complete the task. Thus, a CPO cannot rely on the fact that all stakeholders in the business will accept or agree to all the projects, activities and recommendations that make up transformation, nor will they necessarily provide requisite support within the timeframe of the project when requested.

So, if the transformation project value or the agreed timeframe to deliver is at risk (for whatever reason), the CPO should have authority to escalate issues and seek resolution or direction to assure project success. This assumes, of course, that the role vested authorities are not apparent in the CPO profile. Otherwise, at project end, it will be too late to correct matters, thus compromising value to the business.

Simple organisational mechanisms, such as the creation of a sub committee of the EXCO body, under the authorisation of the CEO and chaired by the Chief Financial Officer (CFO) or the Chief Operating Officer (COO) — i.e., those who have the necessary organisational authority to resolve issues — should be established. Reporting into this group should be weekly and any variance to plan should be identified for resolution. There may be other organisational solutions but as a minimum, project reporting should be frequent and escalation for issue resolution should be integral to the process. This is discussed again in Chapter 7.

CHAPTER 3

Procurement Strategy

The word *Strategy* may sound daunting to some, but when you break it down to its constituent elements, it is not as difficult as the word suggests.

Essentially, a strategy, particularly a procurement strategy, is about four key elements and they are described below. In summary, these elements can be converted to **four leading questions** that require deep reflection and will require analysis, research and syndication within the business:

- *Where* are we now? We need an honest assessment of our current position, performance, constraints, blockages, and how we compare against our peers. It will answer the *why* question as it will show the current level of performance and highlight the potential.

- *Where* do we want to be? This may be as simple as presenting the opposite view of where we are today. It should be aspirational but realistic. It should also represent big step change/improvement, be exciting, and importantly, one that aligns with the strategic business direction and one we are promoting to the company's CEO/Senior Executive Team. In this section, we can answer the *when* we want to achieve this outcome.

- *What* do we have to do to get there? This is the hard part and will describe actions and key changes that will be introduced. In short, it answers *what are we going to do, what are the first steps, what has to change?* We may include here the *who* as in who will be accountable for delivery.

- Lastly, *how* do we measure our success, measure progress to reach our goals and milestone dates?

It can be presented on a single page as follows:

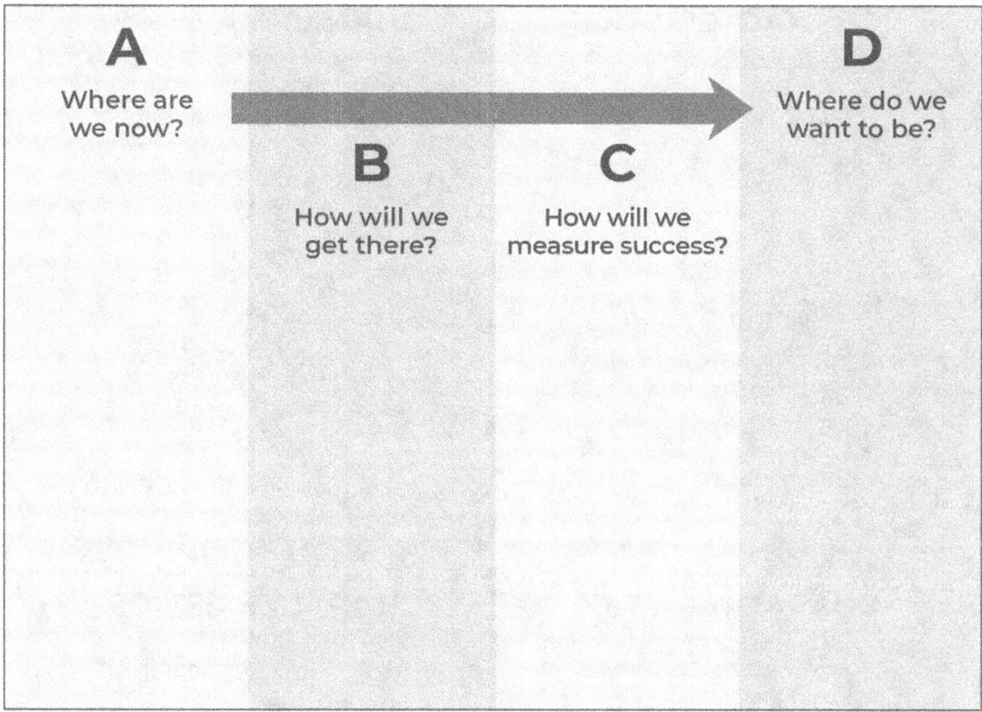

Naturally, there will be a number of supporting pages that feed into this summary.

The information that needs to be gathered for the development of a strategy includes:

- 'current spend' profile analysis, showing where we spend our money, by whom, with whom, and on what

- supplier profile — number, annual spend, largest through to smallest; once done, a useful way to understand your supply base and their impact to the business is to classify suppliers into the following four quadrants:

SUPPLIER PROFILING
Alignment with Transformation Objective

CHARACTERISTICS

- Some large value contracts critical to business
- Alternatives exist in market

Renegotiation

- Align with Transformation Objectives
- Secure terms that are affordable

CHARACTERISTICS

- Very few suppliers
- Supported by existing contract
- Negotiated Pre-Transformation Commencement

Strategic Renegotiation

Align with Transformation Objectives

CHARACTERISTICS

- Low value and commodity type spend
- Competitive Market

Consolidate

Consolidate to a manageable number, secure by contract (one-page RFP)

CHARACTERISTICS

- Alternatives exist in market
- Supply essential to business
- Redefine CAC, align with business strategy

One Page RFP to Market

Secure via contract

Maximum 1 month turnaround

- current supplier contract profile — those governed by a contract, those covered by purchase order only

- measures used to gauge procurement performance; historical performance.

- current Value Policy

- team organisation chart, structure, those in transactional roles, those in sourcing, other

- standard documentation, protocols used including number of standard contracts, Tender, RFP, Expression of Interest (EOI), RFI and RTA proformas

- number of Purchase Orders issued, average value and average line entries; note extent of free text

- data (if available) of supply relationships with no contracts, contracts/ POs issued after supply service completed

- contract management performance, contracts reviewed in situ to gauge ongoing performance

- qualitative data on quality of scopes of work, extent of supervision, extent of rework

With the foregoing in place, it provides a performance baseline, and from there, gaps (or opportunities) can be determined, and where priorities in effort should be placed can be identified. Presenting this baseline performance data to senior leadership is very powerful as it reflects the extent of lost value and potential opportunity to the business. It will certainly attract their attention and, importantly, provide their support for change.

The next step would be to interview senior organisation leadership to obtain their views on procurement performance and develop a report card on positives and negatives.

We are then in a position to define where we want to take the business. There are numerous publications on what leading practice looks like. For example, a quick internet search using search words, such as *best practice procurement* followed by a *Tier 1 Consultant's name*, will generate a lot of useful material to help define vision and aspirations.

Engaging Tier 1 consultancy firms to support the definition of what 'good' looks like is one option unless the skills are already apparent in the business to complete the task. Tier 1 consultancies can provide an independent peer review and advise on optimal solutions and pathways to achieve end goals.

However, I find it best when the organisation does the core work above, generates the required data, describes a view where to take procurement within the business, and *then* engages a Tier 1 firm. This way, you lead the engagement and drive the required outcome rather than the possibility of being driven in a particular direction that may not be optimal for the business. The consultancy then becomes more focused.

The definition of 'good' should include Process, Resources, Technology, and Measures as suggested in the following chapters, e.g.:

Process: Outcome focused, simple, aligned with business strategy, key report development, short cycle times

Resources: Capable, commercial

Technology: Digitisation, automation

Measures: TCI, those track strategy development and outcomes; should include End of Line (EOL) performance measures as well as Process-related.

Let me pose a scenario, not an uncommon one, particularly in large organisations.

Let us assume the procurement function is part of a central shared services team, providing a service to all business units, departments and functions but reporting into a Headquarters role. It follows there would be a Service Level Agreement (SLA) between procurement and the business, defining accountabilities, deliverables, and so forth. Measures of performance would be different to a team integrated into the business as procurement under this scenario would have no visibility of client priorities, strategic objectives and, indeed, would have no accountability for Profit and Loss performance.

So, how would that scenario play out in a true transformation program? Where does the incentive lie for procurement to undergo major change, and what role would the disparate business units (BUs) have on the program?

The first thing to say is procurement in these circumstances can initiate and drive improvement at any stage, change or simplify processes and become more relevant to their customer base. I would go further and say it should not only be expected but would be a requirement. The discussion with the BUs under this scenario, though, will be a very interesting one. Interesting because it will expose the minimal impact a team divorced from the business has — in terms of influencing customer's financial performance, truly understand its cost drivers, its priorities, its budget constraints, as quite simply they have no accountability for its financial performance. In short, those in a central Shared Service organisation will have many masters, each with differing priorities. This is not a surprising conclusion because different organisations will have different performance measures, differing agendas and priorities, and operate under different definitions of value.

I would hope that two things come out of this discussion that will significantly improve relationships. Firstly, there is a change in performance metrics, particularly on the definition of value from 'Negotiated Price Reduction after Supplier Bids Received' to TCI. What a difference that will make to alignment of interests, and it will most certainly increase the relevance of procurement to the business unit. The second is to reshape procurement plans away from a Sourcing and Tendering activity list driven by contract expiry dates to a reconstruction aligned with BU priorities. The revised plan then becomes relevant to the BU. In turn, it naturally follows that communication between the two parties will increase, become sharply focused on business performance, and there will be a greater understanding of BU priorities, all of which will lead to an increase in service level. The BU will quickly become impressed with improved client reporting and the impact procurement will have on its key financial metrics. The easy part will be to redraft the SLA to align with real performance drivers relevant to the customer. What an opportunity for a centralised procurement team to undertake!

In summary, the outcome of the strategy work should be a clear statement where you want to take the business, a recognition of where we are today, and a well-developed and supported plan to take you there. Engaging the team as well as the business will pay dividends many times over, as it will not only ensure their support but also create the all-important *procurement pull* to help drive to the required outcome. What is required is a solid fact base that lays the foundation to design a new procurement organisation. The data presented can help alleviate any internal politics that can damage transformation objectives and build a better and more collaborative business with roles and responsibilities clearly defined.

To further help the development of a procurement strategy, the following diagrams and images may prove valuable:

- Key Measures - those that are common to traditional procurement organisations and those in leading practice businesses. In the Bain and Company publication I referred to earlier – *Building a World-Class Procurement Organization* (October 2014, p.7) – I was taken by the following words that bring the key measure of TCI to life: *"It's hard to convince a hard-nosed CEO or business leader of the benefits of a new procurement organization using qualitative terms. What really matters are high initial savings, then reliable ongoing results year after year. In our experience, nothing beats a savings-based case for change..."*

MEASURES

TRADITIONAL PROCUREMENT	LEADING EDGE PROCUREMENT
• % of goods under Contract	• Cash Flow Generated
• No. of Sourcing Programs executed	• TCI Impact generated through Sourcing and Contract Renegotiation
• Value - Negotiated Price Advantage from Lowest Tendered Price	• % Sourcing Programs concluded in 3 months
• RFP / Tenders Issued	• No. of Contracts Rengotiated in Period (Prior to contract end)
• Maverick Spend	• % of Spend Negotiated / Renegotiated in last 2 years
• No. of Evergreen Contracts	

• No. of Purchase Orders without contract;
Issued – <$1000
– >$1000
	• % Suppliers Aligned with
	  – Business Strategy
	  – Business Sustainability Objectives

• No. of Sole Source Negotiated Contracts	• Supplier Generated Value – Innovation, Sustainability, Cost Reduction
• DIFOT Performance Process, Governance & Compliance Focus	• Other measures aligned with Business Strategy and Performance

- Comparison of Procurement Practices adopted by Tier 1 versus Tier 2 businesses; the aim is to demonstrate how a simplified procurement approach can lead to better procurement, essentially *good business.*

PROCUREMENT APPROACHES

	TIER 1	TIER 2
GOVERNANCE	· Prescriptive · Detailed · Process Heavy	· Fit for Purpose · Process Light
MARKET FOCUS	· Price · Process Compliance · Long, Comprehensive Documentation	· Total Cost Impact · Shortened documentation separating Commercial aspects from Governance
MEASURES	· Process Compliance · Transactional · Goods under Contract · Contracts Executed	· Impact to 'Botttom-line' Performance · Contracts renegotiated to align with market / refreshed business strategy
REPORTING	· Customer-centric · Process Emphasis, value generated through negotiations	· Primary = Contract signatory · CEO / Senior Leadership · Impact to Costs and Cash Flow
SOURCING CYCLE TIME	· Rarely measured as emphasis is on assuring best outcome for business	· Concluded sourcing programs in 1-3 months *Aim is to negotiate and renegotiate/refresh spend base once every 3 years (max)*

I respect that many readers may be new to the measure TCI, but to illustrate its importance; you cannot promote a procurement strategy relying on supply-side economics alone. Demand-side economics (volume, service levels and specifications), including supplier lead identification of inefficiencies must be recognised as well.

This is a big departure from traditional models, and its impact in developing a better run, leaner and efficient business can be enormous. If nothing else, it leads to total transparency procurement is providing to the financial metrics of the business.

- Traditional and Leading Practices in Procurement, a view. This can be used in the development of a strategic vision where to take the business.

TRADITIONAL VS. LEADING PROCUREMENT

TRADITIONAL PROCUREMENT

LEADING EDGE PROCUREMENT

TRADITIONAL PROCUREMENT	LEADING EDGE PROCUREMENT
· A service function, respecting the needs of the customer	· A fully integrated team, key customer is contract signatory
· Reliance on Market Competitive Testing (3 Quotes, RFP/Tender)	· Market and Business Conditions drive market approaches based on CAC* Compliance
· Process Compliance	· Outcome focussed to align with Business Strategy
· Strong Governance Controls	· Requisite Governance Controls Verified through company website tab
· Emphasis on Volume Leverage to secure Best Commercial Outcome	· Business input sought prior to Market Engagement for CAC and BATNA development
· Supplier Negotiations Commence after initial market responses	· Compliance with Commercial Award Criteria (CAC) drives Supplier selection
· Commercial Options presented to customer for Acceptance / Rejection	· Negotiations Commence with clear developed strategy including CAC and BATNA
· Category Management - Static	· Market and Business conditions drive commercial renegotiations not contract expiry
· Technology / Paper Based Mix	· Technology-based, digitisation controls
· CPO Reports into Finance	· CPO Reports into a Procurement Steering Committee chaired by CEO or delegate
· Procurement Covers Partial External Company Spend	· 100% of External Spend Coverage reviewed annually for opportunities
· Source Programs take 6-12 months	· All source and renegotiation programs completed in <3 months

The concept of CAC is discussed further in Chapter 5 – Process

CHAPTER 4

Resources

Good business needs good people. By that opening statement, I mean having people capable of executing and completing assigned work commensurate with its complexity.

Transformation is complex work, but it cannot be delivered without the right people. If not, strategies become of little relevance, promises of value delivery become hollow and procurement once again becomes a low-ranking team, one with great potential but delivers little.

A procurement strategy not only needs good people to execute it but also requires individuals capable of delivering significant and measurable commercial value on a continual basis. This extends to influencing, championing, driving and embedding change in the business, possessing a strategic mindset, as well as good analytical and negotiation skills. It requires individuals comfortable in promoting commercial solutions to executive leadership and hungry to align their work with improving key financial metrics of the business.

A summary of the essential skills of procurement team members required to execute strategy leading to transformation would include:

- Strong assertiveness skills through the ability to lead, shape and successfully conclude commercial negotiation activity. With that, an entrepreneurial flair so that creative options can be developed to overcome negotiation blockages or major sticking points

- Strong project management skills to complete work within agreed timeframes and an ability to work to tight deadlines

- Strong analytical skills (e.g., the ability to determine the true profit a supplier generates from a commercial transaction)

- Strong contract development and management skills

- Resilience

- Honesty, independence and trust must also be present, as team members must operate free of influence or bias toward particular outcomes/suppliers.

These skills can be developed, but transformation work and executing strategy can only get underway once the requisite and capable capacity is in place. That capacity can be hired and is a sound approach to follow as execution can begin reasonably quickly. Under this scenario, ideally, there should be one client business resource for each external expert so that knowledge transfer and learnings from the consultant can be rapidly absorbed.

See below for an example RFP that can be used to hire experts from the external market.

REQUEST FOR PROPOSAL
Supply of Consultancy Services

INTRODUCTION

Client context and why the need for services/define expectations.

Our major focus and priority are to simplify all aspects of our business, remove substantial cost, and continue to operate safely.

Within this context, wet seek proposals from capable suppliers for the supply of XYX.

REQUIREMENT

We are looking for proposals from capable suppliers who can assist/support the business through its transformation journey to a low-cost sustainable organisation and meet the challenges of the current economic environment whilst maintaining service levels to our customers. We envisage a four- to six-month consultancy, working at our head office in location X, directly supporting XYZ and working with key members of the management team.

COMMERCIAL AWARD CRITERIA

The award of business to the successful supplier will be based on the following essential criteria and supplier proposals should structure their responses aligned with these key elements:

- Proven and demonstrated experience that you have done this work before
- The ability to mobilise a capable team of capable people to client premises within two weeks from XYZ date ready to initiate the assignment
- Demonstrated ability to work with cross-functional teams and that through effective knowledge and skills transfer, a legacy remains to sustain business improvement
- Alignment of commercial interests (including risk sharing arrangements).

NEXT STEPS

Proposals are requested by close of business on XYZ date (say one week from RFP issue), these will be evaluated the following day, including closing any queries the business may have. Potentially successful suppliers may be invited to present their proposals on XYZ date in person, telepresence or video conferencing technology). The client Executive Committee (EXCO) will meet on YYY date and make a final decision as to business award leading to contract signature by ZZZ.

(E-mail/telephone number) will be available throughout two key dates to answer any queries you may have. No extension to the aforementioned dates will be possible.

This RFP is issued under client's RFP and tender terms and conditions, a copy of which is available at client website (indicate website address). All respondents to this RFP will deem to have complied fully with its terms.

Of critical importance, too, is the role of the leader and to recognise the level of work that the leader should operate. Procurement, particularly procurement transformation, *is* a complex task — one that requires effective skill in communication and influencing. The person must be technically strong in their field, possess commercial understanding, knowledge of the business and a leader must have the drive, commitment and enthusiasm to succeed. The positive mindset of the CPO will cascade into the team to lift their performance and assure business-wide recognition.

At a minimum, the leader should be capable of developing and implementing strategy, working with and influencing boards and those at the Executive Committee (EXCO) level to secure optimal commercial terms for its external spend base. If the CPO is too far down in the organisation, the authority to drive change is reduced, and accountabilities of the leader will be limited to the traditionally held view that the authority of procurement extends to price only and not to all cost drivers such as demand levers, service levels and specifications. The authorities of the role will be diminished and constrained to a limited functional role.

The role of leader cannot be emphasised enough, along with the essential requirement of good leadership to deliver procurement transformation projects successfully. The following additional context is provided.

You may have worked for good leaders in your career and know the difference between management and leadership. Leaders are interested in team members' development, provide coaching, provide intellectual capacity, offer experience, direction, reinforce project deliverables, clear barriers to provide efficient work amongst the team, and much more — all to ensure a healthy work environment with motivated team members. A manager will get things done. A leader carries broader accountabilities to lay the foundations for success, guidance, motivation and has access to top-line business leadership.

There are many publications on leadership, and what I write cannot do justice to the already existing and extensive literature on the subject.

What I can provide based on my own experience on transformation as well as from literature available on the internet are the key and important aspects that collectively deliver successful programs through good project leadership.

These are:

- Leaders should provide team members with clear purpose and direction of transformation objectives so that lasting change results.

Transformation needs to align with company strategic direction so team members can understand the consistency of the project work to strategic goals

- Taking the above one step further, the cornerstone of transformation lies in effective communication focusing on the following:

  - build ownership of the change effort among team members so they are aligned to the project, come on the journey, support its direction and feel ownership in the program; reasons and rationale for change require explanation as well as the *why* and *how* it will lead to a better business

  - project progress requires regular reporting, ideally a weekly update, and as a minimum, to focus on those actions that have delivered success to reinforce good teamwork done and benefits to the business

  - transformation involves a lot of hard work. What is also important is to ensure sustaining activities (i.e., Business as Usual (BAU)) continue to be delivered and done in a manner consistent with progress towards transformation

  - reporting and sharing all achievements, both big and small, across the business; this will shift the focus of the business and provide support for work to be done differently. The positive impact of change to all stakeholders in both efficiency and effectiveness will be particularly valuable.

In support of the foregoing, the following is an extract from a publication by McKinsey & Company, *The People Power of Transformations* (10 February 2017, p.11) that adds a further dimension to the need for quality communication by leadership and the involvement of the Human Resources (HR) team:

- *Show—don't tell—progress to the front line. When large companies embark on a transformation, there is a risk that frontline employees will see only the individual pain and not the aggregate gain. Communicating clearly and creatively in a way that stimulates dialogue around the transformation's ambition and progress further increases the chances of success. Techniques such as regular surveys taking the organization's cultural pulse, and progress parties celebrating a transformation's milestones, can help create a foundation for real dialogue between senior leaders and the front line on the transformation and the potential changes to be made.*

- *Involve HR as a strategic partner. Transformations have a significant impact on employees and therefore require active involvement from human resources. Yet respondents tend to perceive their HR leaders as less critical than other senior roles to the transformation's outcome. For this view to change, the HR leader must set up his or her function to position itself strategically at the centre of the transformation, rather than playing a transactional role. This will allow HR to make full use of its expertise and contribute to the transformation in important ways, such as moving people around the organization—in moderation. One way for HR to add value in a transformation is by taking a clean-sheet approach to the organization's new, post-transformation design, then using strategic workforce-planning tactics (such as recruitment, talent development, and dismissal) to achieve that vision.*

- *Engage employees through new channels...reaching the front line is a greater-than-average challenge at larger companies. But companies of all sizes can benefit from creative, more digital approaches to engaging employees in a transformation. The use of social media, change-management apps or games, and live-feedback tools should support and complement the movement of information from the top to the rest of the organization, rather than replace traditional methods. Such approaches can do so by making communication more tailored and personal to individual employees (for example, sending personalized push notifications if a milestone has been reached) and by providing more regular updates on the state of the transformation. Employees can also use these tools to explore and engage with the changes being made, on their own terms and with the ability to provide feedback. More advanced communication tools will be especially helpful in large companies that struggle to engage the front line and in companies with many different sites or locations.*

Additionally, the following extract from a Boston Consulting Group (BCG) publication on *Transformation: Delivering and Sustaining Breakthrough Performance* (15 December 2016, p.3) highlights the following:

- ***CEOs, boards, and leadership teams need to follow a holistic approach.*** *It's important to plan for and engage in three parts of a transformation:*

  - *Funding the journey. Identify short-term sources of funds, look for quick performance improvements, launch rigorous program to fund the journey*

  - *Winning in the medium term. Work to enable a new competitive position, setting growth targets, entering new markets and abandoning old ones, and changing the business model.*

  - *Organizing for sustained performance. In parallel, transform the organization to sustain the performance. This holistic approach is essential to strong and sustained value creation.*

- ***Leaders need to focus on putting people first.*** *Organizations enable people to contribute, learn, and grow. The best organizations help people find meaning in their work. As organizations transform, leaders need to ensure that they are truly motivating and enabling their people throughout the transformation journey and beyond. To do that, leaders need to stop treating people as a means to an end—or, worse, as collateral damage—and instead start putting people first.*

- ***Successful leaders approach transformation as a journey.*** *Taking the journey requires thoughtful attention to three key success factors: leading the transformation through all its stages; managing change to ensure that the organization is ready, willing, and able to change; and building capabilities for transformation that lasts.*

Additionally, further advice is offered and examines situations in which transformation programs do not work. To quote Jim Hemerling, co-editor of the article (p.4), *"There are many ways that transformation efforts can go astray. Leaders can misstep by failing to link the transformation to the purpose of the organisation. They can set the ambition too low or too high or declare victory too early. Other missteps are focusing too much on efficiency ahead of other measures or failing to sustain the transformation by building the required organisation. And transformations can suffer if leaders make the mistake of treating people as a means to an end—or, worse, as collateral damage. But leaders who commit to transformation and pursue it systematically are more likely to deliver and sustain breakthrough performance."*

Once the *right* team is in place, we can turn to the question of doing the *right* work.

By *right work* what is intended is building and securing the strategic framework for enduring benefit and impact to the organisation. It requires resources with the ability to think and work in timeframes of two years and beyond. Future sourcing activity and commercial contract framework require aligning with business strategy that typically has a forward view of two to five years out. Thus, sourcing needs to shift from seeking best commercial deals from current market opportunities to aligning the supply base with the required strategic business direction. The two may be compatible but the focus is a move from an exclusive view on lowest price to one of commercial competitiveness AND supplier capability to take the business forward. It also necessitates the ability to review current contracts in place and realign with the future vision, determine changes to current processes that are essential to conform to the new business direction, speed to conclude deals, redesign them and implement the new procurement operating model.

Securing the right team is one of the hardest parts of transformation required to achieve desired outcomes. The reason is that inevitable changes to the team may be necessary to ensure a major step-change in procurement's performance. It also takes time. There is no magical formula to secure the right team, as training is only a partial solution. The inherent capability must be in place, so the injection of new skills may be the only viable solution.

External resources can and will provide the required solution. The key question is whether the business wants a sustained solution embedded as a way of working or a temporary one. The key is to ensure the business team has the all-inherent capability to drive and sustain the value transformation can bring.

CHAPTER 5

Process

My experience in business is that it is far easier to design a complex process than a simple one. This might sound strange to some but it is no different from saying that it is easier to write a long report than it is a short one, one that quickly gets to the point, summarises salient aspects and concludes with a clear recommendation. These are skills and are well worth developing. Leadership in business has limited discretionary time and needs reports and information that summarises what they need to know. One does not need twenty pages to justify the depth of work done; one page will do. Their skill set includes questioning and identifying inconsistencies and discrepancies, so discussions and presentations need to be short and focused.

And so it goes for process. I always recall someone in business telling me, "It does not matter what the outcome is. As long as you follow process, we will protect you." That statement may well be reflective of the company culture, but what happens if it is a flawed process, one that consistently gives sub-optimal outcomes, one that consumes an inordinate amount of time, one that includes many non-value-adding steps? Beware those processes that fit into this description and do not be afraid to challenge them.

My contention is to think of outcomes as the guiding principle. There may well be some key steps to observe along the way, such as approvals after a project milestone is achieved or before any significant financial commitment. Still, these are secondary to having an exclusive focus on good outcomes as the end goal.

One compelling but simple graphic I would like to share with you is the Influence Curve.

INFLUENCE CURVE

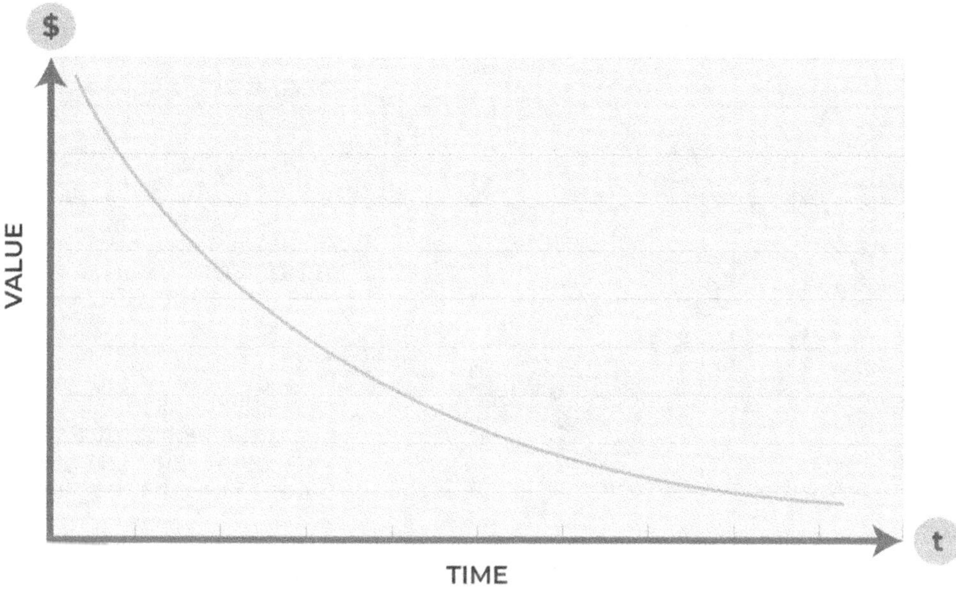

What this curve demonstrates is that the greatest value in any project is in the initial planning of the activity and not at the end. As time progresses, it may be too late to initiate changes, redesign parameters, introduce new assumptions or strategies — essentially, all matters that with careful thought and care would have generated increased project value and should have been identified at project initiation.

To put this another way, if mid-way through a project, it is evident that it is essential to redesign the project to ensure project objectives or deliverables are met, it will not only result in increased project costs but also will add to delays in completion. Project Net Present Value (NPV) will be reduced.

The foregoing provides excellent context to sourcing activities and how the process may be redesigned to provide significant additional value on a recurring basis. A typical sourcing process presented on a linear basis would look something similar to what is shown below.

TYPICAL SOURCING PROCESS

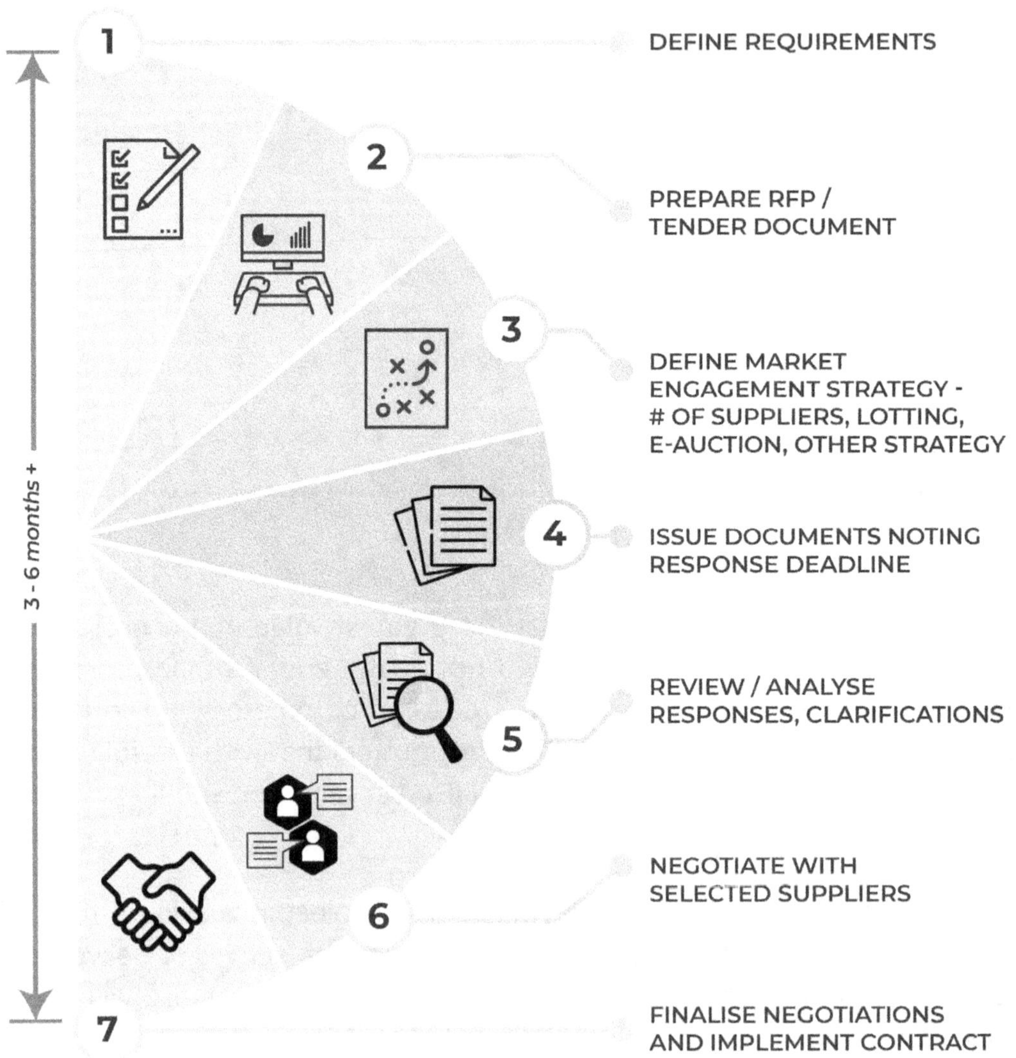

Presented differently and converted into the format of the Influence Curve, it would look as follows:

TYPICAL SOURCING PROCESS

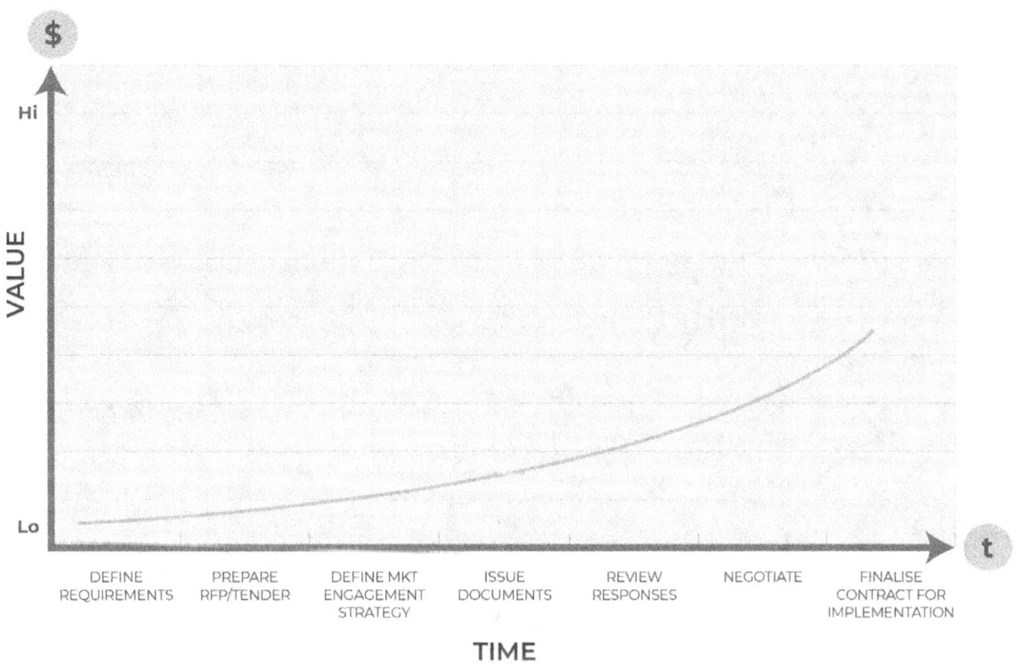

The process kicks off and progresses with a number of low value-adding steps. The major value in the project is confined to the end when negotiations take place. At that stage, maybe due to lack of planning, market understanding, lack of preparedness on supplier profiling, or lack of integration with the business, it may be too late to secure the best outcome for the business. It is why the graphic portrays value achieved only halfway up the *y* axis.

Now let me redesign the process and how this would look re-presented into the Influence Curve.

Redesigned Process:

NEW APPROACH

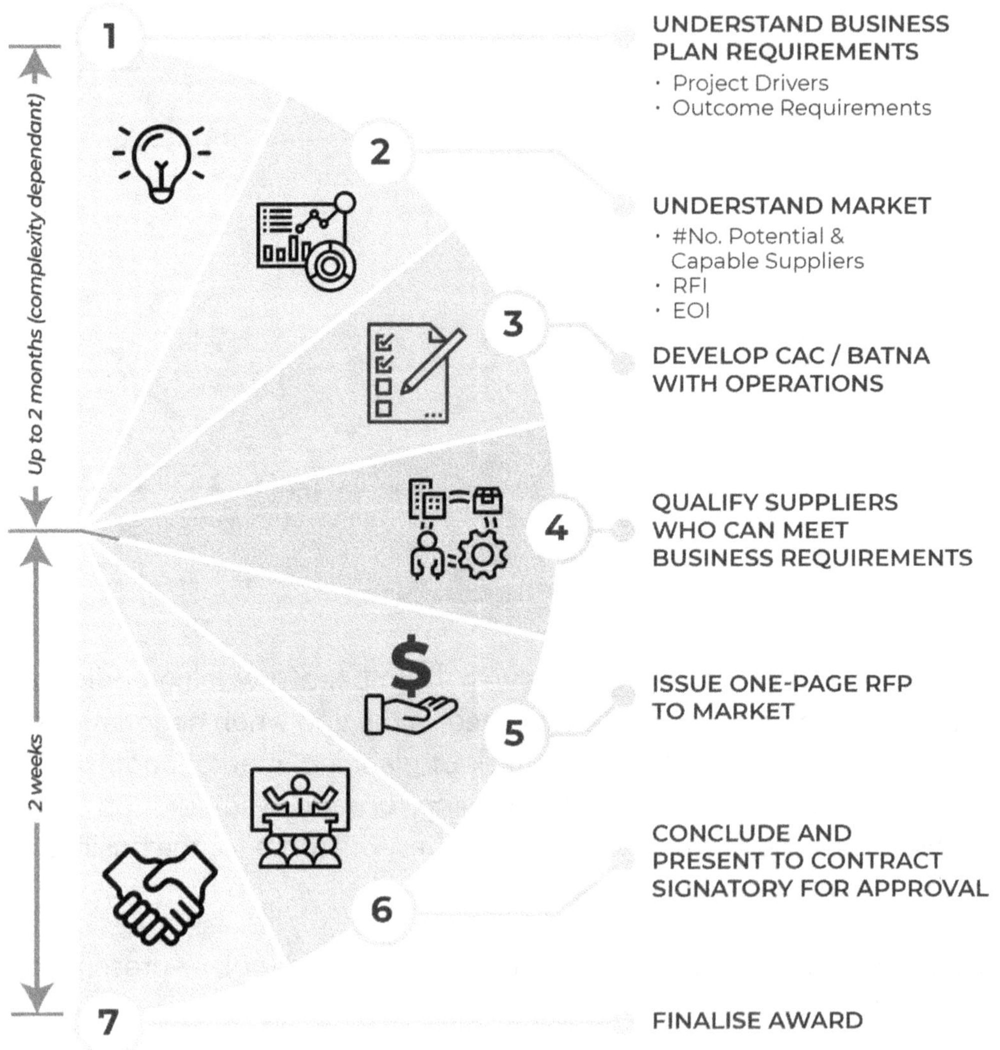

Reflected in the Influence Curve:

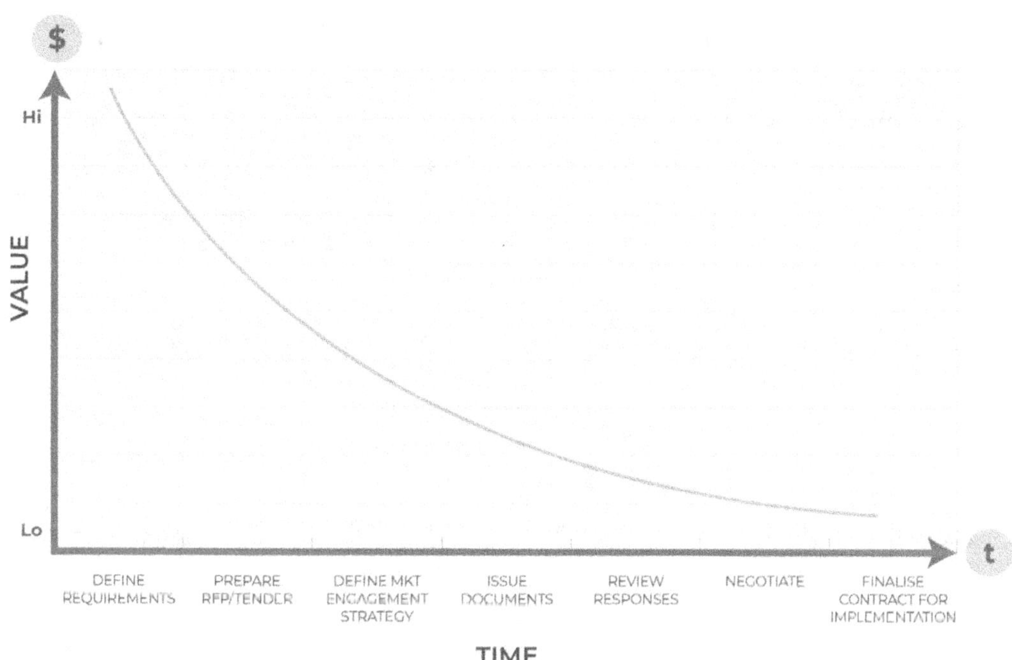

By increasing the effort into the start of a sourcing program, particularly before the initiation of market engagement, the buyer will be substantially more informed of market pricing dynamics and supplier capabilities, which places the procurement professional in control of the process. Tight integration with the business will have been achieved so that their *full* needs beyond minimum service levels and ideal pricing will be respected and factored into Commercial Award Criteria.

In my first book, I devote a whole chapter to the concept of Commercial Award Criteria (CAC) and its importance and relevance to sourcing activities. Rather than replicate it here, simply put, the CAC is a statement on *how* an organisation will award business. It provides full transparency with the supply community. It is clear and leaves the supply base in no doubt what the essential minima are to achieve. As it is a very important topic and is key to achieving a simplified sourcing process, and at the same time raising procurement's commercial and business credentials both internally and externally, a simplified summary in graphical format is presented below:

COMMERCIAL AWARD CRITERIA*

ESSENTIAL CRITERIA	SUGGESTED 'PICK' CLAUSES
· CAPABILITY	· Demonstrated achievements as a supplier that emphasise the compatibility of your skills to complete envisaged work. · The ability to provide a team of capable people to support effective delivery of assignment.
· SERVICE LEVELS	· The ability to meet service levels specified in Attachment X. · Provision of technical support to oversee successful implementation.
· SPECIFICATIONS	· The ability to meet minimum specifications provided in Attachment Y for application abc. · The ability to execute scope of works x and acceptance criteria of z.
· ALIGNMENT OF COMMERCIAL INTERESTS	· A proposal leading to a 30% reduction in TCI to the business from 20xx spend. · A commercial proposal aligned with the business's transformational objectives noted in the preamble to this RFP.
· IMPACT	· Demonstration of a zero carbon footprint strategy in the production of xyz and delivery to our operation. · Clear demonstration Supplier can meet company's sustainability objectives (Att. Y)

* A clear statement to the supply community how the business will make a commercial decision

** Please refer to my book, *Procurement - Redefined, Impactful, Compelling* for a full suite of options for criteria to use

I cannot emphasise enough the importance of investing time in developing the CAC and ensuring alignment with commercial, operational, supplier capability and strategic outcomes. As a further context, other than what is presented in the above image, it is here we can place performance metrics such as environmental and sustainability objectives, say in the case of buying plant and equipment, "use of renewable energy sources," "water and energy efficiency of equipment," "equipment lifetime" ...thus all those that lead to reduced waste generation and lower costs. So, with the context of sustainability etc, procurement can expand the types of KPIs placed in the CAC – which support a supply chain audit where independent assurance of objectives can be shown to the shareholders.

Let me revert to the updated Sourcing Influence Curve and represent it in a slightly modified way expanding on the first step on the *y* axis, namely *Align Procurement Approach*. This is where the real value is derived and is a step often omitted. Importantly, though, in procurement transformation, this is critical, and it demonstrates tight integration of procurement with the business and *why* the measure of value, TCI, can be applied. Represented:

PROCUREMENT / VALUE LEVERS

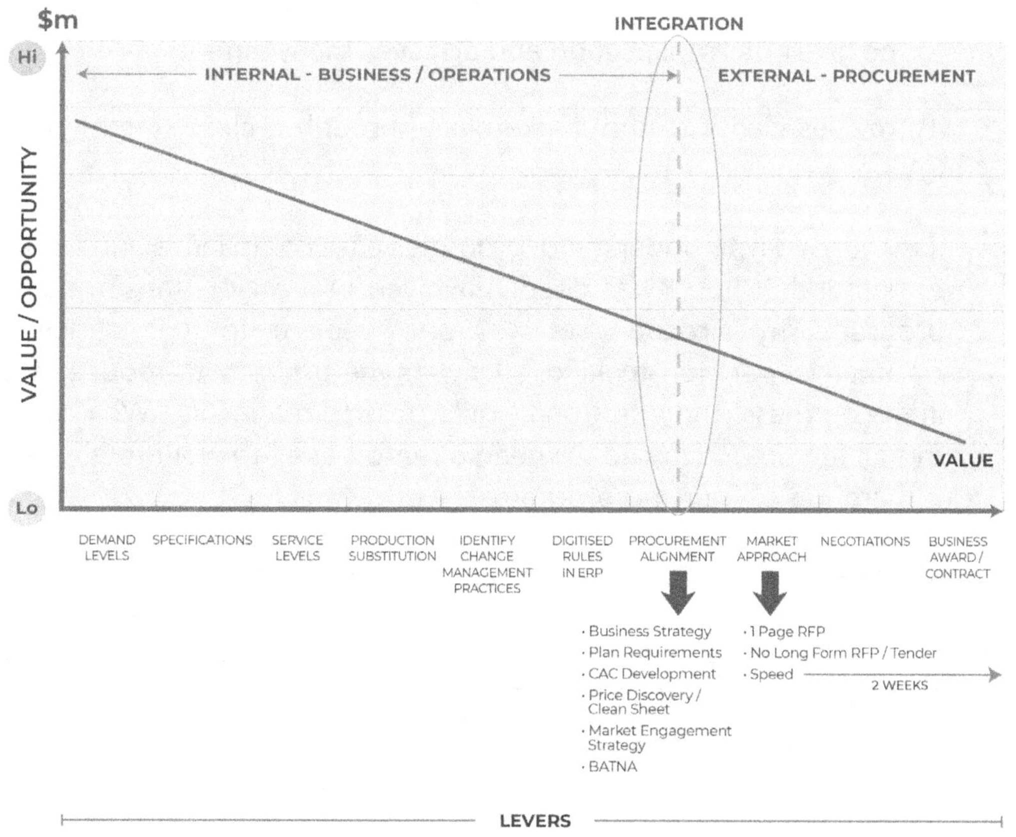

The left-hand side of the column *Integration* shows the typical demand-side drivers that influence total cost. These typically lie within the domain of the business or Operations and fall outside the traditional authority of procurement, namely *price*. The key point here is that leading practice in procurement would approach the market through sourcing programs on a Total Cost basis, and these individual elements are an essential part of developing the CAC described above and, importantly, aligning the business with procurement before market engagement. The developed CAC allows procurement to deal with the market and conclude negotiations directly as clarity and authority have been provided and if the criteria are met, then it can lead to rapid close out of programs.

It also shows that the greatest opportunity in cost reduction does not necessarily come from price but demand levers. Tight integration of procurement with the business opens up a new world and is a cornerstone of transformation.

It does not end there. I present below a format for a one-page Request for Proposal (RFP) document that can be used in all sourcing programs. This is radically different from the majority of long complex ones typically deployed. It gets to the heart of simplification and achieves many aims:

- it provides clarity to the marketplace through a clear statement on CAC

- it is short, easy to understand, promotes easy compliance and a quick turnaround. When I was deeply involved in a major transformation program, my direction set was one week from RFP launch to commercial decision-making, such was the urgency to reduce costs in the business. The question I would pose to readers is, "Why not do this all the time? Why do we need a reason at all to work to a weekly turnaround of sourcing programs"?

- all the essential information required is presented

- it separates our governance requirements from commercial information; governance information is contained on the client's website.

REQUEST FOR PROPOSAL (RFP)*

This RFP is issued under Client's RFP and Tender Terms and Conditions, A copy of which is available at Client website (www...). All respondents to this RFP will deem to have complied fully with its terms.

Introduction:

Requirement:

Commercial Award Criteria:

Next Steps and Timing to Business Award:

Client Availability:

* This document can be condensed to 1 page

** Examples of completed Pro Forma RFPs are contained in my book,
  Procurement - Redefined, Impactful, Compelling for a full suite of options

The same applies to other sourcing protocols, namely Request for Information (RFI) and Expression of Interest (EOI) documentation. These can be neatly presented on one page as follows. The same benefits to the simplified RFP apply to these documents as well.

Examples are provided below:

REQUEST FOR INFORMATION (RFI)
Supply of XYZ

CLIENT BUSINESS AND CURRENT CONTEXT

Business Context, pressures / burning platform. Set the scene.

Our major focus and priority is to simplify all aspects of our business, remove substantial cost, and continue to operate safely.

OUTLINE OF BUSINESS THAT IS AVAILABLE TO PROSPECTIVE SUPPLIERS

Here we would list volumes, timing of expiry of current contracts and also mention minimum qualification criteria that would need to be satisfied to win business (safety, financial strength, experience, ability to meet our needs, adhere to our standard contract (refer our website) etc.).

**DRAFT OUTLINE OF CRITERIA ON WHICH BUSINESS
WILL BE AWARDED AT NEXT RFP PROCESS**

The RFP will contain a clear statement on how we will award business to the successful supplier. They will include:

- Minimum Service Level Requirements including stock holding requirements, quantities, delivery times etc.

- Minimum Specification Criteria (maybe better to specify the application and what we need the goods for / to do, rather than get locked into a straight-jacket / too restrictive a specification.

- Any Technology / Innovation requirements?

- Any key risks we want the supplier to absorb?

- A proposal leading to a x% reduction within 12 months in the Total Cost Impact to the business from 2019 spend of $x (thus including price, demand, specification and service level drivers); in recognition of this, Client is open to consider an appropriate length of contract, a simplified commercial environment, and other criteria that the supplier may wish to propose.

INFORMATION SOUGHT FROM SUPPLIER

This will include company profile data (or reference to website), why they would make a good supplier, confirmation they would be willing to participate in an RFP process and meet key commercial award criteria. We may also ask for indicative pricing for some specified items / services that would be included in an RFP to get a feel for the competitiveness of their offering.

CLOSE OFF WITH FORMALITIES

Who to write to, when, format, openness to consider questions etc.

EOI DISCOVERY TEMPLATE

*Use this document to discover what savings / opportunities
are available to the Business.*

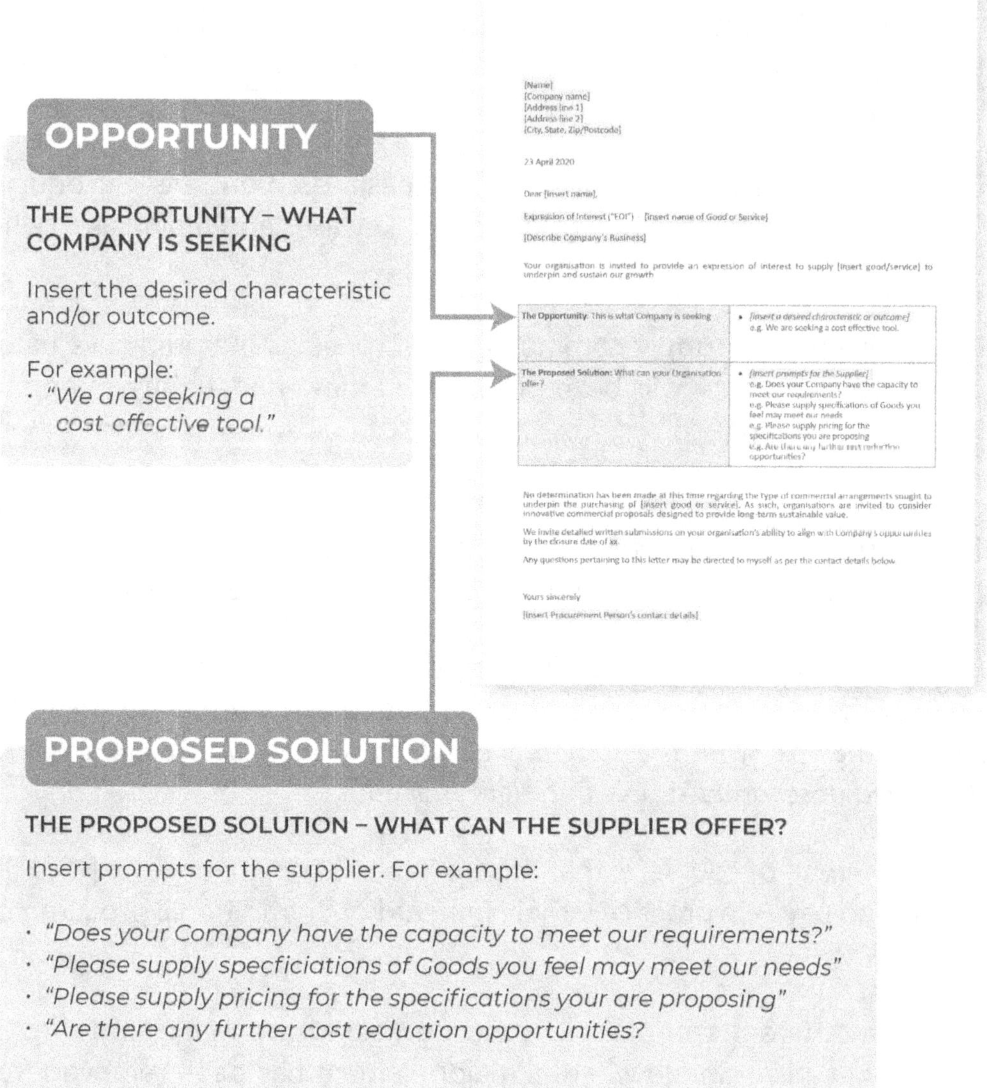

OPPORTUNITY

THE OPPORTUNITY – WHAT COMPANY IS SEEKING

Insert the desired characteristic and/or outcome.

For example:
- *"We are seeking a cost-effective tool."*

PROPOSED SOLUTION

THE PROPOSED SOLUTION – WHAT CAN THE SUPPLIER OFFER?

Insert prompts for the supplier. For example:

- *"Does your Company have the capacity to meet our requirements?"*
- *"Please supply specficiations of Goods you feel may meet our needs"*
- *"Please supply pricing for the specifications your are proposing"*
- *"Are there any further cost reduction opportunities?*

With these simplified protocols in place, the essential tools are there to not only progress procurement to leading practice but also to a transformative approach, resulting in tight integration with the business.

Simplification also achieves:

- lower costs to run processes

- shorter turnaround in receiving information (cycle time) as explained above

- the supply community will be encouraged to respond, as they know they will be making a significant investment in time but only for a short period

- your reputational equity will increase as you are introducing transparency regarding requirements, key asks and timing as to when decisions will be made and

- it will take the supply community by surprise as the predictive nature of requirements will be replaced by a new and tightly integrated business response.

Regarding the point of taking the market by surprise, I came across the following from the *Wall Street Journal* (7 July 2021), which reported an innovative approach to securing products in a constrained market:

Nikolaj Wendelboe, the chief financial officer of Danish electronics company Bang & Olufsen A/S, in recent months has acquired a new responsibility: setting the price range for what the company is willing to pay for semiconductors, a tactic aimed at securing supply in a tight market.

What is different, of course, is that the customer is nominating the price that it is willing to pay — a practice largely unheard of in traditional procurement organisations.

Adopting a different approach to sourcing, taking the market by surprise, particularly in this example where a major element has been removed from negotiation (pricing), will not only shorten the sourcing cycle time but also enhance corporate reputational equity.

Finally, one further process to discuss is that of negotiations. Having a well-developed CAC will certainly simplify negotiations, as the ask is very clear. The supply community knows what is required and how and when the business will make a commercial decision. Having that clarity is valued by suppliers.

All successful negotiations start with good preparation. The following essential information required is outlined in the table below to aid the development of a negotiation strategy. Depending on the complexity or size of negotiations ($ value commitment), the strategy may need to be approved by the contract signatory or higher authority. Having this information ready will aid that process.

One aspect I have noted in my career is how long it can often take to secure a signed contract after essential commercial terms have been agreed to in a source program. This point may resonate with you. It can be driven by several factors, including contract/legal complexity, over-governance, the introduction of new players into negotiations (e.g., contract signatory, lawyers, senior counter party management, to name a few). All of this can lead to potential erosion of benefits, a renegotiation and invariably increased time and effort on the part of procurement.

I advocate that legal contract negotiation is an integral part of negotiation. No handshakes should take place until this is secured. You will be familiar with the expression, "It's not all over until it is all over," and so the real process end is contract signing.

Too often, I have witnessed trading commence while a contract is still under negotiation, and worse, supply market dynamics change, and what was negotiated has to be redone.

My strong advice is to prioritise this activity before resources are assigned to new project work.

NEGOTIATION STRATEGY*

Negotiation Objectives / Outcomes:

Contextual Data / Information:

- What is under Negotiation
- Counterparties
- Size of Spend
- Proposed Contract Term
- Contractual Clauses Remaining to be Negotiated and required position
- Criticality of Spend to Business and Counter party
- Place of Negotiations

- Strengths / Weaknesses - Ours / Theirs

- Proposed Team / Leader / Roles - Ours / Theirs

- Define a good deal and possible trades to ensure outcome

- BATNAs - Ensure approval by Senior Business Leaders

- Prior Work Before Negotiations:

  - Availability of Contract Signatory / Senior Business Leaders during Negotiations

  - Alignment of Key Opinion Leader in Business to ensure rapid close out of deal

* This can be developed in Power Point Presentation

Much has been written on negotiations, and I devote a chapter to it in my first book. The following are the keys to a successful negotiation:

- Be assertive

- Retain control of the process

- Know what you want... ask is clear, put a tight timeframe around it to reach conclusions, make it clear we have a Best Alternative to Negotiated Agreement (BATNA), and are prepared to move. It is MOST IMPORTANT this is communicated at the first meeting, as it is always harder to introduce new boundaries during the process as quite simply more negotiation trades may have to be offered to achieve desired outcomes.

- finally, it is important to remember to conduct a commercial negotiation divorce from establishing or retaining supplier relationships. Too often, I witness negotiations conducted in a friendly manner that should be avoided until negotiations are complete. Sending signals that relationships are a key part of the negotiations sends a soft signal to the counter party and exposes a weakness. There is plenty of time after negotiations to establish requisite relationships.

I have presented a lot of material in this chapter, so let me summarise:

- process simplification drives better procurement practice, resulting in improved commercial outcomes, tighter integration with the business and strengthens your position in commercial negotiations

- procurement transformation is essentially about outcomes, not process compliance

- procurement transformation changes the dynamic from price focus to total costs, and that, in turn, drives tighter integration with the business

- commercial negotiations are an essential part of the process to secure and endure commercial relationships, the key to their success lies in the quality of preparation and execution

- Finally, I present a summary from my first book that summarises the differences between traditional sourcing approaches and those required under a transformation environment, emphasising simplicity of process and placing increased effort at the front end to gain maximum value at process end as illustrated by the Influence Curve.

EXTERNAL SPEND MANAGEMENT

TYPICAL BUSINESS APPROACH

- Heavy / exclusive reliance on process, use of RFPs/RFTs
- Default of competitive sourcing
- Work usually assigned to low levels within organisation
- Value determined as "negotiated price improvements from initial supplier responses"

- Documentation is long, complex, expensive and 'market predictable'
- Price focussed
- Supplier lead responses that set negotiating parameters
- One size fits all

- 'Process compliance' rather than Plan management / business outcomes
- Little work done prior to market engagement

- Risk averse, heavy reliance on specification compliance/retention of service levels
- Operations unwilling to assume risk for commercial reward

- Supplier relationship building rather than cost reduction

NEW APPROACH

- RFPs / Tenders have outlived their usefulness as a tool for supplier selection – the focus is on business bottom line impact after disregarding market price movements
- Total market opportunity/understanding
- Understanding of Plan costs, business drivers, and senior management expectations and assuring outcomes meet these requirements
- Business focus rather process focus

- Process light, emphasis on speed and value capture
- One-page RFPs, RFQs, etc.
- Better use of RFIs (Request for Information) to determine if supplier base suitable
- TCI (Total Cost Impact) rather than price so that outcomes directly traceable to the P and L account

- Much work to be done to align business requirements, customer needs, flexibilities, min/max specifications, risk appetite and importantly, to align the executive team to ensure Plan requirements meet. This in turn provides the authority for Procurement to engage the market and close deals if cost reduction targets met
- A simplified process compliance environment, centred on front end controls

- Development of total cost reduction opportunity, decision making at senior levels; often plant technical specialists (traditionally risk averse) will stipulate their needs. Their input is respected but the contract decision (often based on $ levels) should be made by the CEO

- Challenge specifications/service levels – understand impact to costs of business. The focus is on the business, not on supplier continuity.

CHAPTER 6

Technical Skills and Technology

Procurement is a big discipline. Some universities offer a degree on the subject. Indeed, one of the local universities in my hometown of Brisbane, Australia, offers students the opportunity to undertake a Ph.D. in procurement.

The point of me saying this is that procurement is a very wide subject, there are many specialisations and professionals require a sound knowledge and technical base to function well.

It goes without saying that those in procurement roles need to have a passion for the work, possess strong motivation to succeed, fit the profile noted in Chapter 4 and possess a suite of skills, including contract management, supply chain assurance, category strategy development, and commercial negotiations expertise to name a few.

To be successful, it is not just technical skills that will make a procurement professional successful. It is also a function of doing the right work, consistent with procurement strategy, business strategy, and importantly, operating at the right level consistent with role title. This is explained in Chapter 4.

In this chapter, I will discuss a number of strategies to consider in sourcing spend categories common to many businesses and how, through adopting the correct approach, reduce the spend base through procurement-driven transformation.

The rationale for including this area of advice and knowledge sharing is to impart a level of technical procurement skills to embed in an organisation and sustain transformation objectives. Sourcing is a key part of procurement, and it is here where the greatest opportunity lies to ensure development of optimal commercial terms aligned with a company's strategic direction. By getting it right at the front end, the project benefits will materialise at the end (refer to the *Influence Curve*, Chapter 4). What I share follows a different, more strategic and thoughtful approach to sourcing and is removed from a *one size fits all.*

These are:

- External Contractor Spend

- Maintenance, Repairs and Operating supplies (MRO)

- Other High-Priority Spend Areas, and

- Warehouse Inventory Management.

I will also discuss *Contract Management, Supply Chain Assurance.* Although separate chapters have been devoted to these in my earlier book, I provide additional input to aid the transformation journey. These are two critical areas, not often done well, and they get to the heart of retaining negotiated contractual value and are an integral part of transformation.

Finally, I discuss *Technology* and consideration to objectives and readiness.

External Contractor Spend

Although I do discuss services procurement in my first book and its higher complexity compared to, say goods, this expense is driven by three elements:

- demand (as in the need to have contracting services)

- price (daily or hourly rates) or fixed for the task on hand

- job specification, complexity of work, job supervision, and fit-for-purpose considerations.

Each of these can be expanded further, as explained below, and get to the heart of understanding contractor total cost and, importantly, what controls require to be in place to achieve excellence in practice and lower spend.

Interestingly, each of these levers can contribute 15% to contractor spend reduction when comparing leading practice with poor, i.e., a total of 45% saving.

Demand

Planning and scheduling. Work needs to be planned, resources estimated and a schedule of external labour hire requirements development, so the business knows what needs to be done and when. Good planning aids in two key requirements, namely, the avoidance of expensive costs of unplanned mobilisation and allows adequate time to secure the optimal commercial outcome for the work required with the supply community.

Price

There are three primary ways to cost contractor work, namely 1) time and materials, time calculated on an hourly or daily rate, 2) fixed price and 3) incentive-based contracts that allow for a bonus calculation if work is completed ahead of time and/or under budget. Which method to deploy is a function of the type of work, labour intensity, degree of supervision, ease of cost estimation, clarity on outputs and deliverables. Adopting a competitive source program, opening the business to a number of capable suppliers, offers the opportunity to examine the sharpest and best commercial deal. An RFP structured around the proforma provided in Chapter 5 should be used, placing particular emphasis on evidence of capability to do the work, meet the client schedule and a robust commercial proposal demonstrating their hunger and commitment to completing the work to client satisfaction.

Job Specification and Supervision

Included here are the key elements of scoping of work, ensuring the best resources are applied to the task (the *A*-team), acceptance criteria are well defined, and the business supervises work done to address any issues on hand to ensure there is no waste in the form of idle time or equipment. Scope writing is a skill and one that can be done jointly by the Operations team and procurement.

All three elements described above need to be recognised in any changes to system design, as good planning may go to waste if work is poorly executed and requires to be redone.

Maintenance, Repairs and Operating Supplies (MRO)

This spend category can be a large expense in manufacturing businesses, in fact, any capital-intensive operation. It may not apply to service-related organisations, save for one principle, namely, expenditure profiling (explained below).

My experience shows this is not a spend category that is done particularly well, and I am being very general in my comments. If, though, we are talking about a business undergoing transformation with the aim of large step spend reduction, clearly, a new approach is required. Typically, MRO is sourced on a lowest price only approach, which ignores demand levers, a fit-for-purpose application and a recognition of which items are critical compared to those that are not. Here is an example of how I would profile MRO spend:

MRO PROFILING

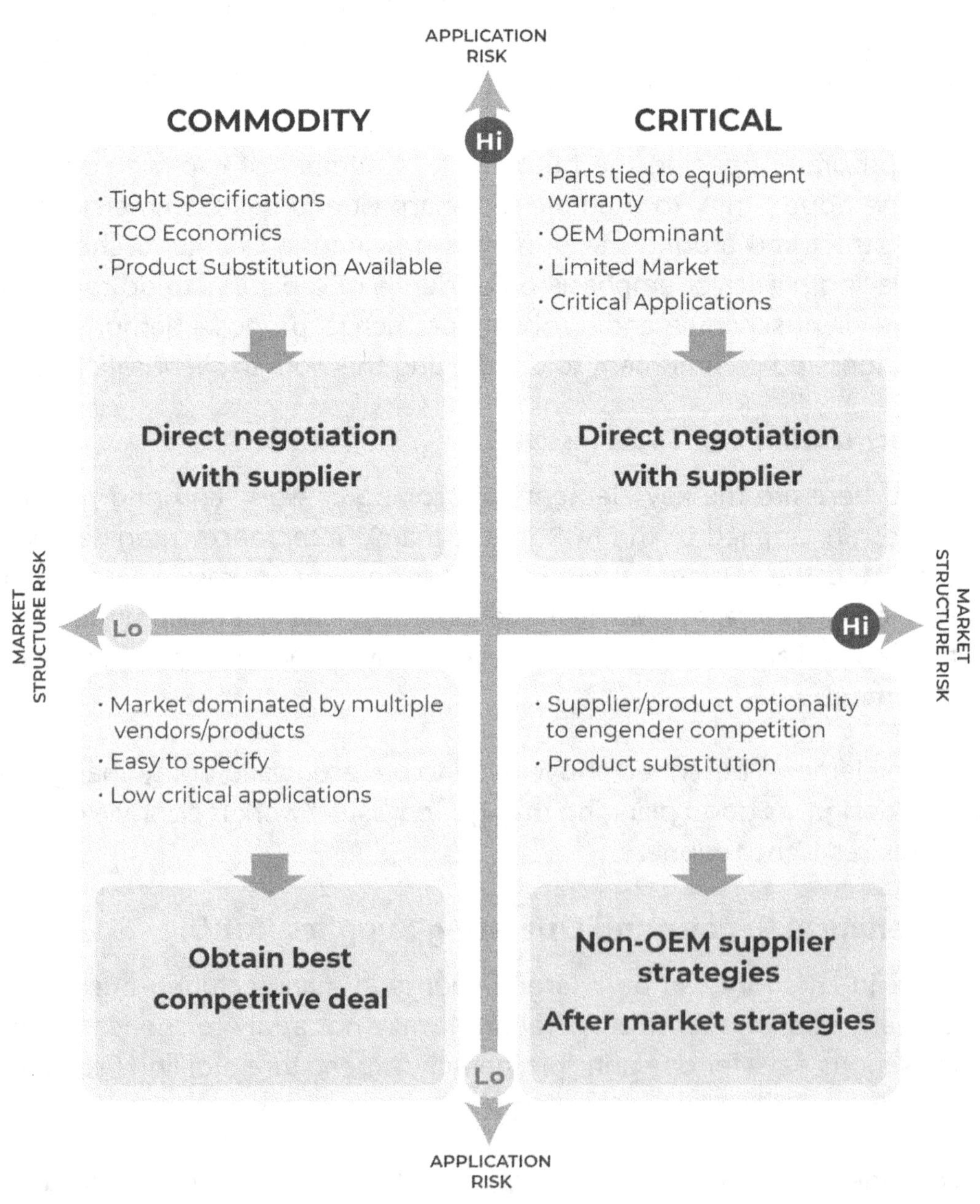

The profiling illustrated can be applied to other spend categories, particularly where many suppliers dominate the total spend, including contractor spend (discussed above), classifying total suppliers within the business, to name a few.

In summary, what I portray in this graphic is firstly to focus on the top right-hand quadrant. These represent items that with strong input from Operations are essentially *non-negotiable,* i.e., the opportunity for product substitution is not open for discussion. We then turn to the top left and bottom right quadrants, which represent items dominated by certain supply market characteristics, leaving the bottom left-hand quadrant for commodity items, where there is much competition and product substitution is readily available.

From there, sourcing and negotiation strategies can be tailored to each quadrant to generate the optimal commercial outcomes.

Other High Priority Spend Areas

In addition to the above, there are, of course, other high expenditure and priority items common to many businesses. These get to the essence of two important points that sit behind *good practice* in sourcing. These are:

- knowing *how to buy;* and

- having a clear strategy supporting the spend area

Both of these together place the buyer in control of the sourcing process as, by necessity, they demonstrate a deep understanding of market fundamentals underpinning the spend category, they align with company strategic direction, and the outcomes required from the sourcing program in question are clear.

A good starting point, therefore, for any business is to classify your spend profile consistent with that displayed in Image 5 but modified slightly as follows:

SPEND PROFILE

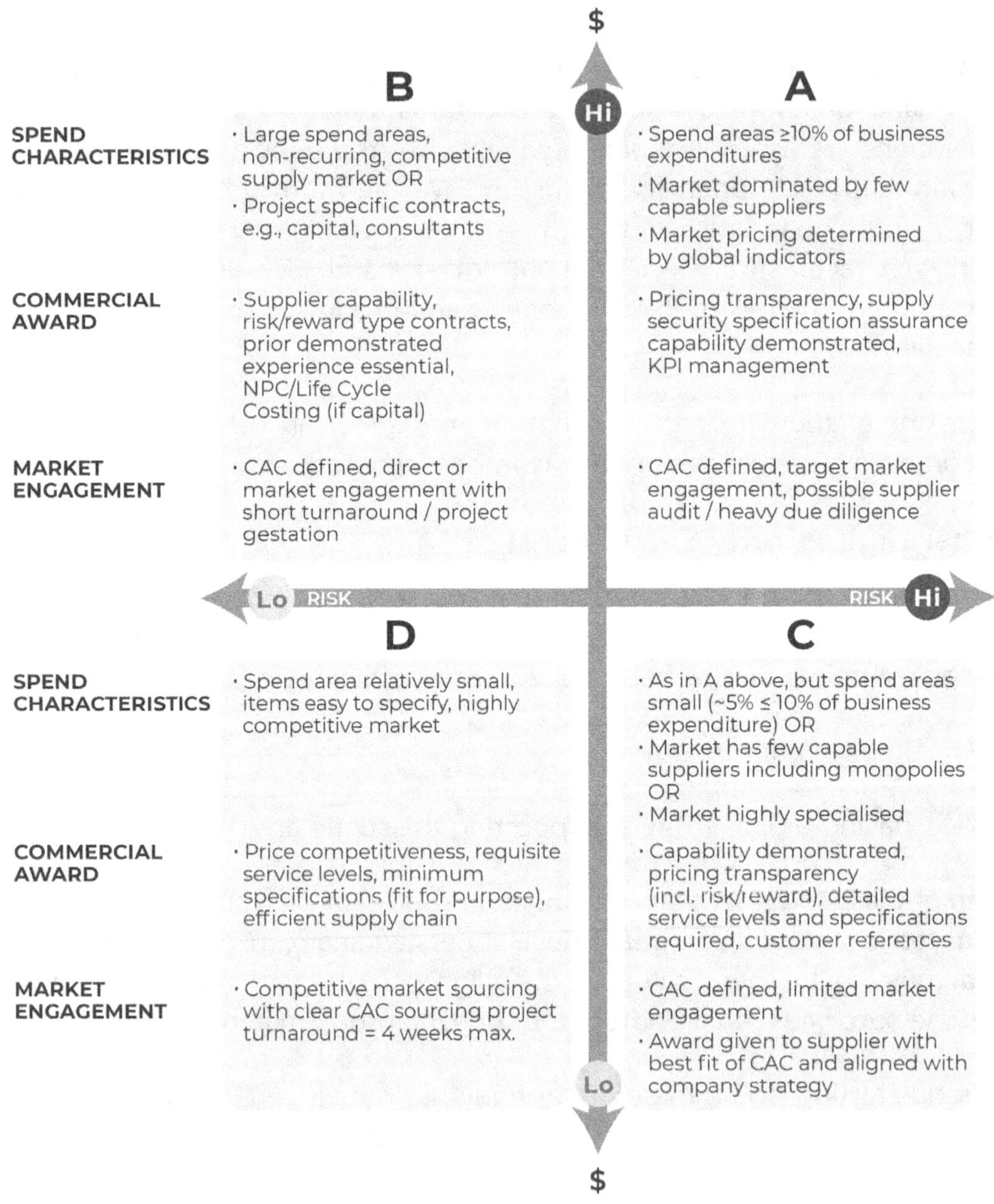

Naturally, prioritisation should be given to those in quadrant A. Much less effort is required for those in quadrant D, where the risk is less and supplier options are great. What this graphic demonstrates is that one size does not fit all. In other words, I have witnessed standard tender and RFP documentation applied to all four quadrants, when a much more simplified approach, especially to those expenditure items in quadrant D, would be applicable. Also, the emphasis on all spend items, regardless of which quadrant they are in, should have appropriate CAC defined and applied (refer to Chapter 5) as securing a good commercial outcome, not just about lowest price, rather the ability to secure terms based on a number of key elements is important to the business, including TCI. In particular, to align CAC with business strategy, supplier capabilities, operational needs and priorities.

Some spend areas include:

- Direct Spend areas such as Raw Materials, Fuels, Transportation costs (inbound and outbound); these may fit into quadrant A noted above

- Indirects such as Consultant and Professional Services, facilities costs; these may lend themselves to quadrant B or possibly C or D depending on spend levels

The assumption I am making is that those in quadrant A are big expenditure items where it is worth the investment in effort and preparation to managing these sourcing programs. On top of that, this quadrant, in particular, is where constant vigilance should be paid to identify any supply chain risks or material changes to market dynamics so that counter risk strategies can be implemented quickly. With devoting time and energy, it will pay for itself many times to ensure the best sustainable commercial outcomes are obtained and aligned with business strategy.

This is in contrast to low spend and commodity type items where a more simplified approach can be taken, and *price*, followed by *service levels*, would be the key determinants of commercial award. The aim for those in quadrant D, because the items are simple to specify, is to complete these programs within a short turnaround period (less than a month) which can only be delivered through a simplified approach, as noted in Chapter 5.

Although the emphasis is on achieving superior commercial outcomes, it would be wrong to leave this discussion and ignore the key requirement for all suppliers in all quadrants, which is to meet essential supplier capability requirements around alignment of sustainability objectives, environmental and safety performance.

Taking these spend items in turn:

- **Raw Materials** – In manufacturing and production, these are critical, not only because without them (supplier outages, supply chain disruptions) you can quite literally stop a plant from producing, but also the quality of the raw material input can directly impact the specification of the manufactured output, important for marketing products. So, two important dimensions to consider in any commercial arrangement with these suppliers would be to prioritise supply chain assurance and raw material specification in the body of the contract, and a third critical area is, of course, price. Quite often, and what makes this spend more difficult than others, is that there may be few suppliers in the market and they may be overseas-based, adding further complexity.

  What is required for supply assurance is a *force majeure* clause, where the supplier takes on the onus of sourcing products from alternative sources in the event of supply outages or curtailments or offers alternative product specifications and allows the customer plant time to modify their processes. If a supplier cannot accept these terms, then developing a secondary, alternative supplier would be essential and thus a two-supplier strategy to support the business. With specification, assurance would be sought to ensure testing is done before shipment to assure requisite quality at source. Variations outside an acceptable specification range require both advance warning to the customer and possible financial compensation. Thirdly on price, a formula-based arrangement often works best as it introduces transparency and works for both parties. For example, inputs can be linked to external markets (say, oil for petroleum-based products), exchange rates, and, additionally, a manufacturing fee. Supply security, price and specification are the three most important aspects of these types of contracts. They are, in fact, for many supply contracts, and the buyer should be well-prepared on commercial options for these three dimensions rather than relying solely on market-based responses.

- **Fuels** – The three essential criteria as noted for raw material contracts apply here as well. In practice, it is a relatively straightforward purchase. The challenges come in fuel specification to meet plant and environmental standards, ensuring adequate on-site storage for supply security and logistics optimisation, and considering the location of source refineries to minimise shipping costs. Of interest, though, are options on price. Apart from index-based mechanisms linked to terminal market pricing, many suppliers offer price hedging, which can be valuable to ensure budgetary constraints are met.

- **Transportation Costs** – For land-based transport, there is usually a healthy and competitive local market servicing this category giving the buyer choice, thus quadrant B classification. Price, of course, is one dimension, as would be safety considerations, reliability of service, quality and size of operating fleet. On price, this is a category that lends itself well to the concept of *clean sheet costing*, i.e., building a supplier's costs from the ground up, including estimates such as price of trucks, annual maintenance costs, fuel, and so forth, to which a margin can be applied. That should result in fair market pricing. If there is major variation to estimates under this methodology compared to supplier offerings, then it opens up an important discussion around *why* this is the case. It may well be there are flaws in customer costings, equally it may expose high and unsustainable margins on the part of the supplier. In short, it places the buyer in control of the process.

For **sea freight**, this is a much more complex spend area, and pricing is dependent on many factors such as shipping volumes, frequency of shipping, load and unload port configurations. It is a transparent market. Global indices do exist to base pricing; however, there are many more considerations. Products can be shipped in containers in bulk, depending on the products shipped there may be specialised ships required, size and type of vessel is a key determinant of price, and shipping contracts can be arranged on a Contract of Affreightment (CoA) basis, time charter or using market spot availability. There are then Incoterms (International Commercial Terms) to consider, which dominate all shipping contracts.

Furthermore, shipping contracts can be secured by the supplier or the customer depending on where the best leverage sits. Engaging a shipping broker is one consideration, more often, though, if this is a big spend item, having in-house shipping and logistics expertise is the optimal way to go. Price is one important consideration as are defining service levels and minimising supply chain risk through shipowners' safety procedures and quality of crews. There is much to say on this category. What I write is a light touch on the subject. Suffice to say, if this is a critical spend area, expertise is required, whether internally or externally sought. If it is a small spend area or one-off in nature, then a supplier lead response may be sufficient.

Further to what I have written on *price* above, you may be familiar with the 'dead band' concept in price negotiations, particularly where product pricing may depend on exchange rates, raw material pricing changes, or other uncontrollable market price movements. Simply put, customers do not necessarily want negotiations to take place daily, weekly or even monthly every time there is a price movement, as these can go up or down daily. The concept of a dead band is to agree the parameters when such a renegotiation should take place (say, +/- 5% of original contract price) as well as the duration over which the market changes are evident.

The concept can be applied to many contracts, as many developed countries have shifted their manufacturing base offshore and now have increased exposure (both favourably and unfavourably) to uncontrollable factors.

As supply chain disruptions have been all too evident over the COVID period, I suggest consideration to this clause to not only ensure fair pricing but also to assure supply of goods and materials should there may be a major change to supply or demand-side economics.

- **Consultant Spend** – Engaging Tier 1 or 2 consultants lends itself well to a simplified source program (quadrant B) based on four essential commercial award criteria:

  - demonstration of prior and similar work done, as well as results achieved; details of specific Intellectual Property (IP) or unique capabilities to underpin value delivered

  - ability to mobilise a team, quality of people assigned to the work evidenced by CVs, capability, experience

  - ability to work in cross-functional teams, work at all levels with the client

- alignment for commercial interests, including risk and reward sharing arrangements

Notwithstanding the fact consultant spend can be very large, engaging the market on these essential criteria will not only simplify the sourcing program but also lays the foundation for a speedy closure and appointment process. Using these criteria is very often sufficient to ensure a differentiated response capable of making a quick response. What goes with this spend is essential project management discipline, as 'scope creep' is very common and requires tight cost control, aligned with agreed deliverables.

- **Professional Services** – this would encompass such items as legal, tax, financial, insurance, and engineering services and fit into quadrants B or C. The cost of these is one important consideration, but just as important (and some would argue more important) is the quality and impactfulness of the advice provided.

My experience in these areas is not to focus on price alone for the key lever for decision making as to supplier selection but considering alternative structures, e.g.:

- it may be that given the wide range of specialisations that exist in these spend areas (particularly tax, legal, and engineering) is to focus on individuals or particular firms that offer the best expertise and then to have a separate negotiation with each. Lower rates can be achieved if firms know they have an exclusivity over certain services and, of course, should be a key lever to apply in discussions

- another way is to approach the market on a wider basis but to seek responses to criteria based on the lines of Consultant Spend above, for example:

  Seek firms that can convert their offerings to spend strategies such as the development of a tax strategy and how they would go about such work for the benefit of their client. The key is to demonstrate the value firms can offer to expertly manage the spend, minimise it, and have a sound risk management strategy supporting their advice. Similarly, with insurance services and conversion of that to a spend strategy, such as consideration to risks, exposures and determination of suitable protection for each identified risk against likelihood of event occurring and what should be self-insured. Ultimately, there will be a trade-off between cost and risk protection. For legal services, consideration to a governance framework, development of standardised contracts for recurring services as well as legal firm engagement protocols to focus on specific areas of advice required.

The list is not exhaustive but suffice to say, careful thought, diligence, development of sound CAC, and market understanding will pay dividends many times over as it places the buyer in control of the process.

Warehouse Inventory Management

Not all businesses have a warehouse of goods and materials (just as in MRO spend discussed above). I cover this area in my first book, but I believe it is an area that warrants special attention in that a) it is usually an area managed by procurement, b) there is often a significant financial investment (working capital) tied up in it, and c) the resultant inventory holding is the outcome of good and bad buying practices upstream in the process. There is often significant waste evident through over-investment or great expense incurred to airfreight or transport-critical items that should be there but are not. These items can stop production and mobile fleet can become inoperative, so having availability to these essential items is of great importance to a plant. Well-developed strategies for critical parts are a crucial component of transformation. Rather than repeat what I have written in my first book, the following is a summary of excellence on warehouse inventory management practices that can help teams in their transformation journey.

INVENTORY MANAGEMENT

TYPICAL BUSINESS APPROACH	NEW APPROACH
• Warehouse Inventory Value is the key driver of working capital efficacy	• Focus is on stock turnover, months' inventory on hand • Deploy leading indicators that show build up of stocks, manage suppliers to perform and cut delivery times • Publish inventories below critical reorder levels • Publish inventories that exceed say 6 months supply on hand and develop counter action plans
• Customer service Levels and "pleasing the customer"	• Customer interactions on stock-outs and over investment • Root cause analysis • Change/reduce re-order levels • Manage inventory as a key asset
• DIFOTIS (Delivery in Full on Time and in Specification)	• Lead time management and supplier improvement • Understanding lead times and their minimisation is fundamental • Supplier selection and reward based on delivery performance
• Minimising Storage Investment (to conserve capital); this includes raw materials	• The size of storage is irrelevant – the number of months inventory on hand is critical as is integrating forecast plant demand, usage, quantities on hand and supplier lead times
• Inventory has low priority within leadership of organisation; accountabilities are usually unclear, 5S* an underutilised tool	• Assign accountabilities and authorities, utilise 5S, inventories owned by site GM

* 5S = Sort, Set in Order, Shine, Standardize, and Sustain

Of significance, the measures and reporting indicated on the right-hand side are transformational in that a) they are rarely applied, b) promote sound asset management, and c) through close attention to inventory holdings, costs will go down as requisite holdings will be in place and avoid expensive supply chain costs to address outages of critical parts.

Contract Management

Too often, this is a discipline that is not given necessary priority. Procurement teams are often too focused on managing sourcing programs, and the performance of existing contracts is often ignored or forgotten. Suppliers will soon fathom out the degree of control a business pays to contract management, and if none or very little, they may quickly adjust to slackened standards which then becomes the new norm.

Contract management has three distinct levels of work, the first of which is more transactional and is carried out reasonably well. The remaining two, especially the third, are rarely executed.

Level 1: refers to contract administration tasks such as processing invoices, compliance with contracts, authorising payments after goods receipt, and day-to-day communication with the supplier. This is essential work and maintains the drumbeat of the business.

Level 2: refers to work such as managing agreed key performance indicators, reporting variances, arranging and holding supplier review meetings, examining areas for improvement, discussing any changes required with the supplier, ensuring supplier obligations are met and generally extracting full value from the contract. Good relations are maintained and are a priority of the interactions.

Level 3: builds on Level 2 but goes further. This level holds the supplier to account for full contract performance and compliance. Exceptions are escalated to senior supplier management, if required termination notices are issued and/or corrections are required to be put in place with due compensation to the business, supplier personnel are fired if deemed to be incapable. Further, information demands on the supplier may be issued (product and shipping details), supplier lead efficiencies and improvements would be the expected norm from the supplier, and regular report cards would be issued to the supplier against these standards (as described above). The relationship is a professional one but the lead business resource would be firmly focused on the organisation's interests.

Leading practice would require all three levels to be in place. One key procurement metric would be "Suppliers Terminated through Poor Performance," another "Contractors whose contracts were not renewed after term completed," signalling the business is open to change and has no preference or bias to those where good relationships may exist at senior levels.

Supply Chain Assurance

This is a critical area which if ignored, can stop a plant from operating or cease production. This aspect falls within the remit of procurement to manage and requires an advanced skill set to assure the business.

Seen at a transactional level, it is a straightforward task. Goods and materials are ordered, transported and delivered. Traditional procurement reports on Delivery in Full on Time and within Specification (DIFOTIS) routinely fall under Level 1 type tasks (under Contract Management). It is, therefore, a rear mirror measure as it reports events that have been completed.

The more challenging work lies in taking a forward-looking view using predictive analysis as well as leveraging current events, trends and prices into assessments and conclusions. If shortfalls are predicted, then counter strategies need urgent development as well as authorisation to implement. For example, events such as:

- collapse of an exchange rate

- social and civil unrest

- military juntas

- severe or extreme weather events

- change in a country's regime, political, economic, leadership

- sudden rises or collapse in commodity pricing

- fuel shortages, scarcity of ocean-going vessels

- a global pandemic such as COVID-19

can have a flow-on impact to supply of goods and materials. It may be goods become scarce, prohibitively expensive, tariffs may be imposed, should these events become apparent, it may be appropriate to stockpile certain goods, alternative supply sources may have to be sought, forward cover on exchange rates may have to be organised.

The point is to identify the risks, report them, develop counter strategies and present these to business leadership for approval and implementation.

At a macro level, the above scenario played out during COVID-19, particularly where dependency was placed on companies operating in overseas jurisdictions, resulting in shortages of many products.

Technology

Businesses today cannot operate without computerised systems, and that includes procurement. What I mean by technology in a procurement sense, particularly with regards to transformation, is automation and digitisation. The technology field is boundless and is worthy of a book in its own right, including such aspects but not limited to the use of Artificial Intelligence, key report generation, advanced risk analytics, and many providers specialise in these offerings. It is only fair I leave those discussions to the specialists.

Before I go deeper into the field of technology, at a lower level and one easier step to implement is developing a Procurement tab on the company's website. Company procurement policies can be included as resources, along with standard contracts, supplier compliance questionnaires (e.g., Health, Safety, Environmental, Finance and Supply Chain aspects), and one with visibility to the supply community. As noted in Chapter 5, this can enable simplified sourcing programs to be executed as suppliers can self qualify for participation in programs and allows for shortened, more commercially focused RFP documentation.

The key success factor lies in preparation (as it does in most things) when it comes to automation of Purchase to Pay systems, and with that, the readiness of the business to implement automation. As with achieving the objective of procurement transformation, it is about change, and change will impact people as processes will be different.

In summary:

- the first step would be to document the present system as well as the new; a good understanding of current pain points is required, value drivers to be evident in the new, and once objectives are clear, the right selection of technology can be made. A best practice vision may be a useful starting point in where to take the business or elements of it.

- once the appropriate technology is selected, the next step would be to develop an implementation plan as it is in this step that engagement and support with the business are essential. A good understanding of the impact to the business will be required and that is the primary leverage to develop a clear communication plan, enlist support, consider timing and transition to the new, the impact to the external supply base and finally, to define measures of success to monitor the change journey.

- the other key step is to ensure the organisation is ready from a technology perspective; such aspects as data cleansing (supplier information, catalogues), a task not to be underestimated, and then to ensure that integration with existing systems is achieved, including bandwidth considerations.

Investing time in these areas will be well worth the effort.

Digitisation goes one step beyond automation of processes, including the ordering and payment cycles; rather, it refers to the whole procurement cycle. Apart from having electronic controls to support process and resultant increased efficiency, a key benefit of digitisation once fully embedded is that it survives changes in team structure and staff turnover. Of course, digitisation does not replace human skills, but it does embed process control points as well as steps that do equate to best practice, such as driving contract reviews, sourcing activities, and more.

The following graphic from *AT Kearney* (modified in greyscale to fit this book) summarises this very well and places it into context with the evolution of best practices in procurement:

EVOLUTION OF
BEST PRACTICES IN PROCUREMENT

In the evolution of procurement, digital is the next wave

1980s ● STRATEGIC PROCUREMENT

· Globalisation calls for a more sophisticated approach to manage third-party relationships and risks

· Frameworks emerge to make procurement more effective (for example, A.T. Kearney's Seven Steps for Strategic Sourcing and the Sourcing Gemstone)

· The rise of enterprise resource planning systems allows for more automated planning, ordering, receiving, invoicing, and payment processes

1990s - 2000s ● E-PROCUREMENT

· Software tools to computerise procurement emerge, including eRFX, eAuction, spend cube, eContract, and eCatalogue

· These tools are used to create, process, and store procurement data

· The establishment of category management and supplier relationship management frameworks create a means for comprehensive supply management

· Procurement's role is elevated from transactional management to strategic sourcing, but the focus is still on cost management

1990s - 2000s ● DIGITAL PROCUREMENT

· Advanced analytics and data-driven optimisation are leading to better insights, allowing for increased cross-domain value-chain interactions

· Artificial intelligence along with relevant insights from other value-chain stakeholders are transforming procurement

· Down-stream procurement activities are being transformed by automation tools, which drastically improve efficiencies

· Procurement moves to the center of value creation by connecting the business with a network of external partners to create new business models

How far and fast a business wants to proceed down this pathway is a strategic decision, but these technologies are available and will soon be considered the norm.

In a recent publication by Deloitte, *Deloitte Global 2021 Chief Procurement Officer Survey* (23 April 2021, p.20), they make the point strongly for investment in next-generation technologies:

"Investments in advanced digital solutions are a key enabler for success. But which technologies are high performers investing in? High performers are 4-5 times more likely to have fully deployed advanced analytics / visualisation, 10x more likely to have fully deployed Robotic Process Automation (RPA) solutions, have fully deployed predictive analytics capabilities and are 18x more likely to have fully deployed Artificial Intelligence (AI)/ cognitive capabilities.....Strong digital capabilities can help procurement organisations improve data visibility and the ability to collaborate/synchronize with suppliers, enabling greater agility..."

Note that an internet search on leading Tier 1 consultancy firms will show many developed papers on procurement digitisation, and I do not promote one firm over the other. All are reasonably consistent with their analyses, conclusions and client offerings. They all present a compelling vision and one where business readiness is a key requirement before adoption. Full implementation can revolutionise the work of procurement, automate tasks, simplify work and create huge efficiencies.

A business can still achieve transformation without full-scale digitisation. In fact, depending on where a business is on the journey of best practice(s), a 'one step at a time' approach is considered best. In that way, it becomes evolution, not revolution, and the step changes to full digitisation become easier to adopt and manage.

In summary, a technology roadmap requires development so that there is a planned and structured approach to technology adoption.

CHAPTER 7

Communication & Reporting

Communication and reporting is a skill that requires development and one which, if done well, will win much praise from peer groups, team members and executive leadership.

This chapter aims to advise on effective communication, particularly when reporting into the senior executive team. At the outset, I will say I am not an expert in this field. I am not here to replace those specialised consultancies that can provide a service far superior to mine. I can, though, outline what is important to this group of people and communication protocols that align with their needs and expectations.

The first thing to remember is that these individuals are time-poor. They are exceptionally busy, have a wide range of accountabilities, have many priorities, and need to sort out the most important task out of many. With that acknowledgement, if we want to access this group, hold their attention, make decisions, then protocols need to respect this, be short, impactful, to the point and be clear on decisions required. By inference, there is no time to prepare for long presentations, showing substantial detail. One useful tip is that if long content is unavoidable, send material out as pre-reading before the meeting, but only talk to one key page in face-to-face discussions. That will allow the senior executive group to consider the content, prepare for questions and allow the presenter not only to deliver the key messages but also have quality access to business leadership.

The next important point is to respect the work of their role. By that I mean if you take the role of a CEO, they are focused on business performance (Year to Date, Forecast for Year, future and strategic opportunities, profitability, cash flow, cost reduction, to name a few), so what is presented must align with their interests, their metrics and what procurement can do to improve them. Therefore, transactional information metrics, typically monitored by procurement to gauge supplier performance, would not align with this requirement.

Below are examples of reports that do work and meet this requirement.

These are:

- Recommendation to Award...two examples

- Monthly CPO Report

- Monthly Tracking of Progress towards reaching Transformation Goals

Recommendation to Award

This represents the culmination of commercial sourcing activity and is one that procurement should be proud to report. It represents the value the team has secured and aligned with business strategy.

The first image is a graphical representation of a reconciliation of the old cost base to the new, showing the individual sources of value generated and negotiated through a typical sourcing program.

COST REDUCTION OVERVIEW

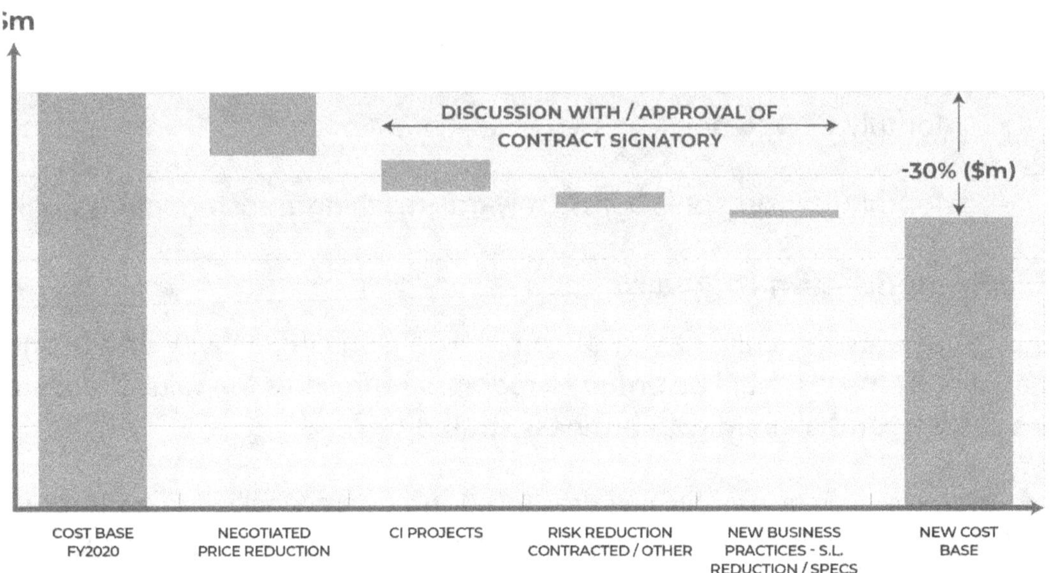

NOTES

· There will always be price reductions –
  1) Use of burning platform
  2) Reduction of Supplier Margins to Fair and Reasonable
  3) Use of Commercial Award Criteria (CAC)
  4) Baseline contract review

· Boxes are not necessarily of equal size (referring to cost downs) other headings
  may be more relevant

· 30% is the target minimum – we can go higher

· CI = Continuous Improvement, projects to be front ended to year 1 in contract
  (money now)

· SL = Service Level

Apart from an easy to read and descriptive report, there are two other key aspects to highlight:

- note that I have illustrated the value generated to be 30%. That is a big number, and it will undoubtedly attract the attention of senior leadership. It is, though, a percentage consistent with transformation objectives. It is also a number that includes all value sources such as price and demand-side levers

- to achieve a transformation type cost reduction may require a level of risk absorption, change in supplier, or some other new aspect to be developed in the supply chain, including product substitution. It may be there is a level of resistance to these changes from Operations. However, the contract signatory, such as the CEO, may well be incentivised to accept the 30% reduction in exchange for risk and for which they carry the ultimate accountability. In this scenario, it demonstrates the contract signatory is prepared to absorb the business risk and will override recommendations from technical and front-line operational roles. Thus, procurement should never hold back from presenting such an outcome, especially in a transformation environment and also given the incentives provided meeting TCI targets.

The second report below presents the same outcome differently, and I have copied this from my first book. It goes further in that it describes some process aspects and a fuller appreciation of the total business impact.

RECOMMENDATION TO AWARD (RTA) TEMPLATE

Recommendation to Award Template

1. RECOMMENDATION

1.1. The Recommendation

Summarise the proposed recommendation. Key inputs include:

a. Who is the recommended supplier, what is the contract for (i.e. what goods or services will they be supplying), when will supply take place, what are the anticipated savings. (TCI basis)

Examples of a recommendation are:

b. "It is recommended that Supplier ABC be awarded a contract for the supply of [Insert Product]. Estimated savings will be $X compared to last year and $Y for forecast expenditure this year";

c. "It is recommended that Supplier XYZ's existing contract for the supply of Maintenance Services is extended for another 2 years, as this will support the business in further reducing costs with a proven supplier. Anticipated savings are $X per annum against planned expenditure."

1.2. The Benefits Summary

a. Impact to Business

Articulate how the business will benefit by implementing this recommendation. Why you think this is a 'good deal' for the business. E.g. summarise how your recommendation compares to the results of your sourcing exercise. This may involve a comparison of financial or non-financial criteria;

Examples of business benefits include:

1. Cost savings;
2. Cash flow improvement;
3. Existing capital optimisation;

Key area to highlight: How will the business benefit by implementing this recommendation? *If financial benefits, keep details brief and make sure there is a cross reference to the Economics section below, where you will provide further information.*

b. Economics

The recommended option's costs, how this compares to status quo, the results of the sourcing exercise and the indicative cost savings to the business (i.e. cost reduction, cash flow improvement). How do you know the preferred option is a good price (i.e. comparative responses during sourcing exercise)? What is forecast target cost savings under this option?

Key area to highlight: What is the savings potential and how is that calculation delivered? What does it mean to me and my business?

The Recommendation

Summarise the proposed recommendation. Key inputs include:

- Who is the recommended supplier?
- What is the contract for?
- When will supply take place?
- What are the anticipated savings? (TCI basis)

Example recommendation:

"It is recommended that Supplier ABC be awarded a contract for the supply of [Insert Product]. Estimated savings will be $X compared to last year and $Y for forecast expenditure this year."

The Benefits Summary

Articulate how the business will benefit by implementing this recommendation and state why it is a good deal for the business. Summarise how the recommendation compares to the result of the sourcing exercise. This may involve a comparison of financial or non-financial criteria.

Example recommendation:

- Cost savings
- Cash flow improvement
- Existing capital optimisation

Both are acceptable.

Monthly CPO Report

This one-page report tracks and summarises procurement activities in the preceding month, highlighting where the input and approval are required by the CEO and their senior executive team. As it is one page, it is easy to read, contains all the essential information relevant to senior stakeholders, and because of its strategic content, it will be read.

CPO REPORT

PARTICULARS		COMMENTS / REFERENCES
A. Contracts and Supply Chain		
1. Contracts awarded in week X Total Annual Contract Value	6 $20m	New Contracts: 3 Renegotiated: 3 Process Compliant: 100%[2]
2. Contracts under negotiation requiring PSC input	2	*Refer Att. 1 for commercial strategy for* **ABC** *Refer Att. 2 for commercial strategy for* **XYZ**
3. Updated executive management summaries for category management strategies	X Y Z	*Att. 3* *Att. 4* } *How macro factors are* *Att. 5* } *impacting the business*
4. Supply chain assurance: those supply chains at risk		**Sole source supply:** Att. 6 **Financial stress:** Att. 7 **Other:** Att. 8

B. Financial	Week X	Forecast Q2
1. Negotiated savings from contracts awarded[3]	$	$
2. Cash generated (incl. price increasae deferrals, price reduction, supply chain savings)	$	$

C. Decisions/Actions required by PSC	No.	Ref.
1. Negotiation Strategies	3	✗
2. BATNA Approvals	2	✗
3. Supply Chain Assurance		
– Stock Pile X	1	✗
– Specification Relaxation	1	✗
– Introduce New Supplier	1	✗
– Increase Insurance Spares	1	✗
4. Price Risk Management	1	✗
5. Early Contract Terminations		
– Supplier Performance	2	✗
– Changing Market Conditions	2	✗
6. Resourcing	1	✗

1. *Distribution: CEO, CFO, COO*
2. *Following competitive engagement process, duly approved by appropriate level of authority*
3. *TCI bases*

Monthly Tracking of Progress Towards Reaching Transformation Goals

This can take a variety of formats. The first example below is more relevant for tracking a business transformation program. Equally, it can be used to illustrate the value generated by procurement in key business metrics of costs and cash improvement as well as initiatives or projects due for completion in the short and near term.

BIAS TO ACTION

We introduced a bias to action and tracked our progress

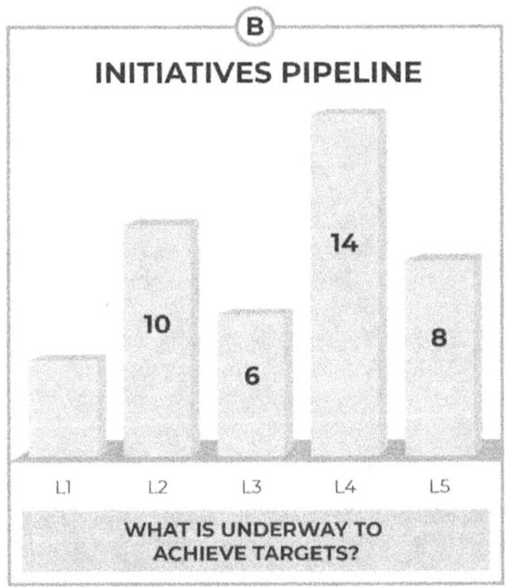

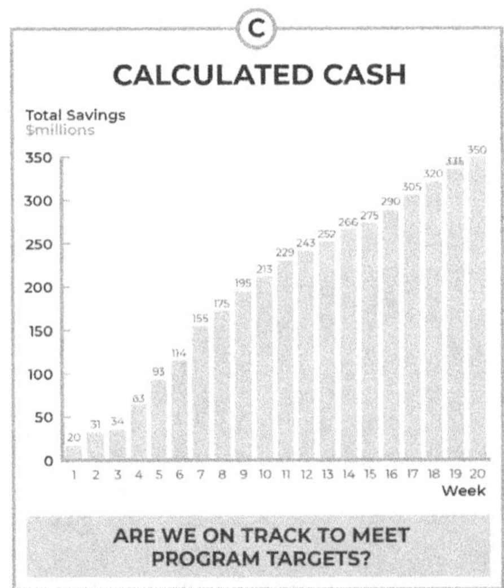

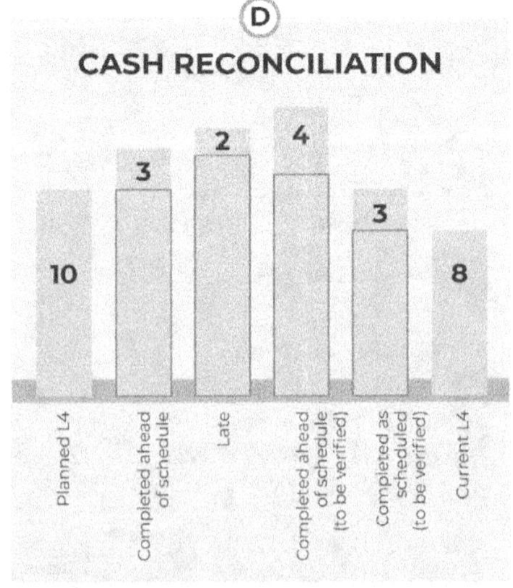

- Daily performance management meeting at category level
- Weekly meetings of CEO and top team to make binding spend reduction decisions
- Relentless "hounding"
- L1 - L5 refers to the status of Initiatives, L1 an idea only, requires analysis, L5 refers to a signed and implemented contract

The second is one that simply lists the target outcomes that procurement transformation will bring, showing progress year to date, forecast for the year, and commentary, whether the initiative is on track or input or direction is sought from senior leadership. Again, this can be developed onto one page. It may be useful if and when a 'red dot' is required (meaning, direction is sought) to succinctly describe what guidance is required.

PROCUREMENT TRANSFORMATION REPORT

TRANSFORMATION LEVER	OBJECTIVE EOL MEASURE	PROGRESS TOWARDS GOAL	STATUS (G) (R)
Protocol Development			
– Sourcing	Developed		
– Contract Pro Formas	Introduced	Complete	(G) (R)
– Governance	Complete,		
– Value Policy	Available on Website		
Strategy Development & Approval	Complete, Syndicated with Key Personnel	Complete	(G) (R)
Organisation Team Complete	100% Positions Filled	50% Complete	(G) (R)
Value Generated			
– Costs	$ x m 20XX	$ a m	(G) (R)
– Cash	$ y m 20XX	$ b m	(G) (R)
Key Reports Developed & Implemented			
– CPO	Developed & Used	Complete	(G) (R)
– Transformation	Developed & Used		
Key Technologies Introduced			
– Automation	Full automation	50% Complete	(G) (R)
– Digitisation	Full digitisation of PO Process	20% Complete	(G) (R)
Category Strategies Developed			
– Top 10 Spend Items	Complete and used	20% Complete	(G) (R)

(G) Green = under control, no issues to report

(R) Red = not on target, senior executive input required

CHAPTER 8

Conclusion

Now that I have walked you through the change journey to achieve successful procurement transformation and all that it requires, it is appropriate to reflect on what has been written before and emphasise some key aspects to ensure success.

As I am sure you will appreciate, procurement transformation is hard work, and there is a lot to do. It takes dedication, perseverance, resilience, faith, and above all, a singular focus to achieve the end goal. It requires leadership, energy and drive. Rome was not built in a day. Typically, one should allow up to a year after the journey commencement to see the full fruits of labour. 'Labour' may be the wrong word in this instance because it is an enjoyable journey, and the outcome is well worth the effort. It is by no means impossible; it is not like climbing Mount Everest, where chances of success are limited. It is a commitment you have made to yourself and the organisation's leadership to transition to leading practice. With every step completed, the light at the end of the tunnel becomes greater and greater. If you are going to invest in the effort of embarking on transformation, you should go the whole journey. The rewards and benefits are what make the journey worthwhile — from a career standpoint, higher status within the business, job satisfaction, seeing the impact of improved financial metrics reflect in the organisation, to name only a few. As I said at the start of the book, it is, in summary, *good business*.

Transformation is about:

- change

- adaption

- open mindset

- simplification (process, governance, less bureaucracy)

- discarding old, out of date practices

- sharper, better, more impactful communication

- redefining relationships (up, down, across)

- passion

- commitment and drive

- leadership

So, let me ask the question, "We're interested and committed; what is the first thing we should do?"

I will answer the question, but first, we need to get a level set, namely, what is our baseline performance, and how quickly do we want to get to the end state transformation? These will have a significant bearing on immediate tasks. Questions that have been posed to me include, "I want to get to the end state and achieve leading practice, but I do not have a team capable of delivery. What should I do?" Another, "I want to get to the end state, but I do not want to terminate any employment in the team, and further, I want to do this without engaging the CEO. Can you guide me?" Another one (different, but related as the drive for major change was confined to too low a level in the business and required the support of all business groups in the organisation to be successful), "I want to reduce my MRO inventory levels, how can I do this acting within the authority of my role?"

The answer to these questions is simply, "I would put aside transformation as an immediate goal and focus on Continuous Improvement. That is, prioritise instead on small step incremental changes that fit within the authority of your role. Once the benefits can be demonstrated, you have a clear case to approach your leader and request increased resources to take your team's performance to the next level, which may include the aspiration of transformation."

But not having the depth of necessary resources should not be a red flag if the drive is there and support may be forthcoming from the organisation. Temporary resources can be hired on a contract basis, or existing resource(s) can be taken out of their roles for a defined period to redesign processes, set up tracking and reporting structures to prepare for the journey, albeit the time to achieve full transformation may take a little longer than benchmark performance.

In Chapter 1, I introduced you to the transformation model presented in a circle, that in summary, says it all. Ideally, it needs either a burning platform to generate or initiate the change or some other driving force where there is a realisation change is necessary, due to sub-optimal performance relative to peers or market trends, for example, or to support a major improvement initiative in the business.

Here is what I would do as initial steps in the change journey:

- get your baseline performance clear

- know and accept deficiencies, inadequacies, gaps and accept any negative feedback as a positive signal, "this is what we must turn around," it sets the agenda as well as some immediate priorities to address

- align the team on the current status, gaps in performance and instil a sense of excitement where to take the team/the business

- get the team involved in setting a new vision/standard of performance; note that if transformation is the objective, it may well be advisable to invest in bringing in a facilitator to ensure outcomes meet the required objectives

- at this juncture, you should have enough material and input to develop a strategy, syndicate findings with Operations and Finance, and use their input to modify or adjust key aspects. The final document should then be drafted in a format for presentation to the CEO/Executive Leadership and then follow the process steps noted in Chapter 1

- it may well be that there is a skills deficiency, so that should be addressed; this is where the help of your leader and/or Human Resources team should be approached. As there will be a complete suite of redesigned roles to support the new transformed procurement organisation, those existing team members should have the opportunity to apply for new roles. Those that are unsuccessful can be reassigned or leave the organisation in a respectful way

- with the requisite organisation in place, support from senior leadership is apparent, redesign work can take place, and from there, the journey begins.

If I reflect more fully on the contents of this book, there are three important points to stress in this closing chapter to ensure we set ourselves up for success. These are:

- leadership — the requisite traits of leadership are discussed in Chapter 4, and importantly, they not only drive the team to success but are there to support change processes and instil a change in mindset away from process to outcomes

- the team — getting the *right* resources at the *right* level to do the *right* work; and

- communication and aligning content and delivery to the target audience

Of course, everything in the book is important. These points, though, can be undervalued or not prioritised, but they are the three fundamental pillars to underpin project benefits. My experience demonstrates if you get these three aspects right, lots of other change priorities fall into place.

On procurement leadership, this is the foundation block to drive and implement change and requires someone who can command the respect of the CEO and their direct reports.

On the second point and complexity of work, redesigning processes, influencing and driving change is complex work, particularly if a tight timeframe to deliver outcomes is a necessity. This work cannot be delegated to too low a level in the business and ideally should be led at Manager level or equivalent. They can be project or contract resources, but the work requires a level of authority and presence to gain the necessary support to implement changes. The key, therefore, is not to underinvest in hiring experienced resources, and secondly, ensure they are up to the task. And with what I have said, their work requires scoping, clear accountabilities, authorities, and outputs noted, and timeframes for deliverables at the required quality set. Placing effort into this task will be well-rewarded.

On the question of communication, this is an area where everyone can benefit from expert tuition. Avoid:

- long-winded PowerPoint presentations

- an unimpressionable presentation - no clear message, asks, direction, conclusion/next steps

- ineffective delivery (lack of passion, commitment in the voice, monotone).

We have all been exposed to these at some stage or another. So, presentations need to be:

- short

- to the point

- have a strong opening line/sentence, so the audience gets involved and excited

- sets the context, explains the problem, describes the opportunity, benefits/value, risks, and implementation plan and next steps

- impactful

- conclude with the opening statement and purpose of bringing the audience together and be clear on asks, help required/seek direction

Above all, the presentation, and as I note in Chapter 7, needs to align with the level of work of the most senior level in the audience. If the presentation is to the CEO, they will be interested in major impacts to the business financial statements, increased shareholder value, major positive changes to efficiencies that lead to lower costs and a procurement strategy that delivers significant and measurable financial benefits. Getting presentations in the required format and content takes practice, as does rehearsal in delivering the opening and powerful statement to attract the audience and retain their interest.

At this juncture, there is little more to be said other than wishing you well on your transformation journey. There may well be bumps in the road and these can be navigated. If mistakes are made, they should be acknowledged and corrected. If support is provided through senior executive leadership, guidance will always be there to help the team as the work outcomes are too significant to ignore.

The investment in good planning, with due attention to key success factors, execution and measurement will pay dividends many times over.

INDEX TO IMAGES

LIST OF ABBREVIATIONS

BATNA	Best Alternative to Negotiated Agreement
BAU	Business as Usual
BU	Business Unit
CAC	Commercial Award Criteria
CEO	Chief Executive Officer
CFO	Chief Financial Officer
CI	Continuous Improvement
CoA	Contract of Affreightment
COO	Chief Operating Officer
COVID	Corona Virus Disease, also known as COVID-19
CPO	Chief Procurement Officer
DIFOTIS	Delivery in Full on Time and within Specification
EOI	Expression of Interest
EOL	End of Line
EXCO	Executive Committee
HR	Human Resources
Incoterms	International Commercial Terms
IP	Intellectual Property
MRO	Maintenance, Repairs and Operating Supplies
NPV	Project Net Present Value
RFI	Request for Information
RFP	Request for Proposal
RTA	Recommendation to Award
SL	Service Level
SLA	Service Level Agreement
TCI	Total Cost Impact
TCO	Total Cost of Ownership